CONTEMNED

CONTEMNED

M. LEWIS RYAN

authorHOUSE®

AuthorHouse™
1663 Liberty Drive
Bloomington, IN 47403
www.authorhouse.com
Phone: 1-800-839-8640

First published by AuthorHouse   07/12/2011

ISBN: 978-1-4634-1659-1 (sc)
ISBN: 978-1-4634-1658-4 (dj)
ISBN: 978-1-4634-1657-7 (ebk)

Library of Congress Control Number: 2011911092

Printed in the United States of America

To You

Genesis is the beginning for so many of our lives. Walk with her
and BJ to uncover what it is that you despise.
Will it keep you from Heavens Door?
What happens if you miss the RAPTURE?

Because I Love You

The Truth Is And Shall Always Be What
We Choose To Believe Sometimes It IS And
Sometimes It Is NOT The TRUTH

INTRODUCTION

Sunday Morning Church Service seems to last forever at Love Life Center, but that's okay, because I am going to sing my solo today. I think it is about time Ricky, the choir director for the last three years, realized that old Sister Anna Mae isn't the only person who can sing. She can't really sing. She just screams at the top of her lungs and some people say she's a soprano. Yeah Right. She is no soprano, alto nor bass. She is the preacher's wife's sister, that's why she gets to sing every First Sunday.

Today's sermon is *The Word of God*. I thought the whole Bible is the word of God. Please somebody tell me this man is not about to preach the whole Bible in one day. I had promised my ex-husband that I would be there to pick up the kids by 2:00PM. Damn. I can't be late again. I am tired of hearing his sarcastic remarks and of seeing the looks on his new girlfriends face. He has gone through so many different women since our divorce till I don't try to remember their names anymore. I just refer to them all as Bimbo Barbie. I think they are bimbos because they actually think being in a relationship with him will last. Ha! The joke is on them and they deserve everything they get for being so stupid. If he was half of a man, we would still be married. But those types of women don't think about the ex-wife until they become an ex-wife.

I have to see my ex-husband every other weekend. Why couldn't I have been a widow? I definitely don't want to listen to him gripe and complain about how my being late is setting a bad example for our kids. He says it shows how little I care about them and he is constantly telling me my responsibility to them as a mother. I had enough of that while we were married. If I could get sole custody of the kids and receive child support without visitation rights, my life would be perfect. I shouldn't have married him. To be honest, I really don't think my oldest is his kid, but that's neither here nor there because someone had to be the father.

Look at what Angela is wearing. You know she looks a hot mess with that red dress on. It's so low cut in the front. You would think she was getting ready to breast feed a baby and it is so short till . . . Well, I better not go there, I am in church.

Oh my God! I can't believe she is about to sit in the front row. How disrespectful can she get? That is the same outfit she had on last night. Obviously she didn't have enough time to change clothes from whomever bed she slid out of. She is such a slut. She gives all good Christian women a bad name. She should have left the club at a respectable time like the rest of us did. Watch her end up pregnant again. Oh wait! It's time for me to sing my solo. Pay attention now Sister Anna Mae and hear how _I Praise You_ is supposed to sound. It should sound like an angel whispering in God's ear and it should be as anticipated as a wanted first kiss. The piano is starting and my cue is coming . . .

I just want to praise~ your~ name~
Oh thank you Father . . . you stopped~ my~ pain~
You lifted me up, took away my cup
And carried my sins to the cross.
You rescued me~~ when~ I was lost
And I praise you oh lord all day long~
I sing praises to you oh lord~ in my song~
I praise you oh lord~ all day long
It's your love my God~ that makes me strong~
And I praise you
I praise you
I praise you
I praise you
I just want to praise~ your~ name~
Oh thank you Father . . . you stopped~ my~ pain~
You lifted me up, took away my cup

Carried my sins to the cross
Rescued me when I was lost
And I praise you oh lord all day long
I sing praises to you oh lord in my song
I praise you oh lord all day long
It's your love my God that makes me strong
Your blood controls all I do
I just want to praise you.

Listen to all of them clapping. They don't clap that way for Sister Anna Mae. People say when she was younger that she could pack the church every Sunday just so they could hear her sing Amazing Grace. I guess she is about 90 years old now. I think they clap for her to sit down and stop trying to sing. I shouldn't be so cruel. Everyone knows I am the best singer and I hope someone tells her so she might stop and yet, I wouldn't want anyone to hurt her feelings. Anyways, I wonder why the church pays the drummer and guitar player to perform and not the choir. If the choir can't be paid, then they shouldn't pay anyone. I could use some extra funds too. You know?

Oh, let me be quiet, Pastor Cook is about heat it up in here with his sexy self. If I for one had only met him first, my whole life would be different. Just listen to his voice. You know, I don't even think he knows how over half of his congregation really feels about him sexually. I mean look at him, looking all tall and handsome with that eggshell white linen suit on, as he stands at the alter requesting the church to say Amen. He is everything a man should be. He would never cheat on his wife. His voice is mesmerizing and his gentle smile is a kiss of morning dew on a fresh white lily.

Today we are studying the Word of God and the purpose of His Word. Please open your Bibles to Genesis Chapter 1, and it says:

- God said . . . let there be light. He called the light Day and the darkness He called Night.
- God said . . . let there be a firmament in the midst of the waters. He called the firmament Heaven.
- God said . . . let the waters bring forth abundantly the moving creature that has life. He created all life.
- God said . . . let us make man in our image, after our likeness: and let them have dominion over fish, fowl, cattle, over all the earth, and every creeping thing that creepeth upon the earth.

We have heard these verses cited many times. And too many times we have overlooked the importance of these words. God spoke everything into existence. The power of his words created the world and every living thing within it. The earth was void and without form. God called everything we enjoy and experience, the heavens, the seas, beasts, trees, birds, etc. into being. God said it was good, not evil or sinful, but good. God then created man, both male and female.

The church was very quiet when Pastor said that was the first creation. We were all stunned when he continued. Now, he said, "We are going to study the creation of the Garden of Eden. The Garden of Eden was Gods perfect place for man and the salvation of all mankind he had created."

God said, "Let us make man in our image from the dust of the earth". God seen that man, who he named Adam was alone and thought that it was not good for him to be alone. He caused Adam to slumber in a deep sleep and took a rib from man and created the woman, who Adam named Eve. Woman was created from man for man. Man was created from earth for earth. Everything was created by the word of God. A lot people are becoming confused today about relationships. Laws are being passed to condone homosexuality. God did not create Steve as Adams helpmate. He created a woman, whom Adam named Eve. Let me continue . . .

The garden was full of trees to eat from for nourishment. But God told man not to eat of the tree in the midst of the garden. You know, God had a plan for the whole earth to be saved. As the story goes, the serpent, which we will call *temptation to disobey God* and have imaged as a snake, encouraged Eve and Adam to eat of the tree in the midst of the garden, that God told man not to eat.

Pastor walked around in the church and all eyes were on him. Then he asked in a loud probing voice, "Are there snakes in your garden?"

Yes. Yes! Yes Sir, the church confessed. He continued to walk and speak through the microphone. Everyone was so quiet till you could hear a feather fall on carpet in that church. Pastor spoke softly and firm with each step he took and his words romanced the entire congregation.

Well God had a plan to save mankind in the garden, he repeated, and that plan was "The Tree of Life". The disobedience of man caused a problem. You see, they could not eat of both trees, The Tree of Life and the tree of knowledge of good and evil. So, since evil was chosen over life, the tree of life had to be protected. Now, the Lord God said, "Let us cast the man from the garden before he takes from The Tree of Life."

God protected the way of the tree of life from man by driving man out of the garden, and guarding the entrance with Cherubims and a flaming sword which turned every way. God cursed the ground and from then to now mankind have had to work hard to live on earth. The woman was cursed with increased pain and births. God said, "she would desire her husband and that he would rule over her."

"But God, yes, God", cried out Pastor, "had a plan!" Remember the Tree of Life is actually Jesus, our Savior. The Word of God is Jesus, our way to salvation and our judge.

Let's turn to John, Chapter 1:1

In the beginning was the Word and the Word was with God, and the Word was God. The Word was made flesh, and dwelt among us, full of grace and truth.

- In God was life; and the life was the light of men.
- The true Light, which lighteth every man that cometh into the world.
- He was in the world, and the world was made by him, and the world knew him not.
- Jesus saith unto him, *Go thy way; thy son liveth.*
- Jesus said: *God is a Spirit: and they that worship him must worship him in spirit and in truth.*
- Jesus said: *I am the bread of life: he that cometh to me shall never hunger; and he that believeth on me shall never thirst.*
- Jesus said: *It is the spirit that quicketh; the flesh profiteth nothing: the words that I speak unto you, they are spirit, and they are life.*
- Jesus said: *I and my father are one.*
- Jesus said: *I am the resurrection, and the life; he that believeth in me, though he were dead, yet shall he live: and whosoever liveth and believeth in me shall never die.*
- Jesus said: *Lazarus, come forth.*

Jesus the Son of God was one with God until Jesus held the sins of the world on the cross. God's spirit could not be host to such sin. Jesus felt God's parting when he asked, "Father, why have thou forsaken me?" Once he was resurrected and ascended to his Father, God, reunited were the Trinity, the Father, Son and Holy Ghost. You see Church, the mind, body and soul is a trinity. The mind is the Father, the body is the Son and the soul is the Holy Spirit. The mind instructs the body to do action things and sometimes the body does actions on its own. Let's say for instance you hit your finger with a hammer. The body tells the mind and the mind sends out pain and a message to your soul (spirit) for what type of emotion needs to be felt, joy or sorrow. This is not a hard concept to grasp. It only requires faith and belief in a Savior that has proven his love for you. Faith in a God that loves you so much, that he sent his only begotten son; that whosoever believeth in him shall not perish, but have everlasting life. Belief is something you make real by faith. Believe and you make Jesus real in your life. Things you would not do in the presence of Jesus in the room with you don't do, because he is with you in every room. You just can't see him until you believe in him.

Remember now church. In the beginning, God created the heavens and the earth. He spoke everything into existence with his Word. Jesus is the word. Jesus spoke things into existence. Truly he is the Son of God, full of the spirit of his Father and the Holy Ghost. Word usage in today's world and all through time has built nations and torn down spirits. Words can stunt emotional growth in children, cause prejudice behavior when taught, place a man into the White House as President and mend a broken heart. Words can make you think you're in love and words can cause hatred and violence. The Bible says to control what comes out of your mouth. Let your yes be yes and your no be no. If you are helping others, you aren't gossiping behind their backs. If you are allowing God to lead your way, you aren't allowing Satan to control your moods.

Will you recognize the voice of your Father when he calls you? Are you so wrapped up in material wealth that you are spiritually poor or dead? Do you believe in the Word of God?

The Word of God is Jesus! Only through his name, his body and his blood can you be saved. In the New Testament, Jesus teaches us to pray and walks us through, step by step, the way to salvation. Don't miss out on the best experience of your life. Learn how to live in the spirit, abide with God, Jesus and the Holy Spirit. Find out what true joy is all about. Capture the miracles God has already performed in your life and watch as he really shows off when you become his born again child. Clean out your closets and rid yourself of secrets that have been anchors in your life. As long as you try to hide sin, it continues to rule your life and control your thoughts. Let it all go and let God shine in your life. Be ready when Jesus calls your name or prepare yourself for hell on earth.

Jesus is coming for his children, his disciples, his warriors. He is coming for the faithful believers. He is coming to claim his crown. He is the bridegroom and his church is the bride. Will you be at the ceremony? Look at your neighbor and ask them, will you be there? The word became flesh in order to show you the way to heaven and the way to salvation.

God despises the lukewarm worshiper, going this way one day and that way the next. My mother would use the phrase: Whatever makes your boat float; because, however the boat floated was good enough for whoever did not want to listen to the words of guidance and wisdom that was coming from her years of experience. She cared enough to try to talk to everyone about Jesus, and she was ready for the wedding. She would not however, give up her ticket. Are you going to be there? Don't let your friend make you lose your ticket. Don't let the people on your job, the other driver in a car, your family, your finances nor your heartbroken state of being, make you get scratched off the guest list.

Then Pastor turned around towards the choir and said, "They don't hear me."

"We hear you Pastor!" shouted Brother Taylor.

"Yes sir!" said Brother Johnson followed by the entire congregation with an "Amen!"

The word became flesh. The word that created the heavens, the earth, everything on earth, you and me, became flesh. He was in the garden as The Tree of Life. He walked amongst his people, and they knew him not. How can you recognize the word? Only if you are born again and God abides in you, will your spirit recognize the word of God.

We have been given a second chance church. Now let's eat of the tree of life, our savior and drink the blood of salvation. His plan is to bring us a new garden. Just obey the word and confess you have eaten of the tree with the knowledge of good and evil. Confess your adultery, confess your homosexuality, confess your thieving and lying nature, confess your self-adornment, confess your idol worshiping, confess your abuse of tobacco and liquor, confess your thoughts of wishing death to others (killing), confess your materialism and coveting, and confess your back-sliding. Jesus shed his blood to wash away that sin. Jesus will forgive and give us a new life, never to sin again. Amen.

Reserve your spot today. Get your name written in the Book of Life. Amen. You are part of the only church that counts as soon as you accept Jesus as your personal lord and savior. Get baptized by water and then by fire, the fire of the Holy Ghost. Amen. The invitation is open and the time is at hand. If you were one of those waiting till the last possible moment, well guess what, it's here and now. Come all people. The doors of the church are open, come to the altar of God as the choir sings.

The doors of the church were open so the church could ask for forgiveness and rest in the open arms of our Lord God. I stood up and began to sing *Yes Lord*. Only two teenagers came up for prayer. We were all looking at each other. Really I think only the three mothers of the church understood the sermon. All that stuff about eating of the tree and dying. Adam and Eve did not die. Plus when we do something wrong, the church would be closed because I think at least half of us here have eaten of that tree. "You know what I am talking about." I think God despises the lukewarm worshiper as Pastor said.

I am trying to remember just what did Pastor say about the rapture two weeks ago. Jesus is coming back for the church. The dead has to rise and then Jesus returns to Earth to fight Satan and collect the Christians. I think that's what he said. I don't know. It is all so confusing to me. Anyhow, I do my part. I come to church every Sunday. Here comes Sister Doris. She is a lying biddy.

Hey sister, how have you been?

She was my friend four years ago, until she was trying to raise money for the Sunday school. She was selling slices of cake that looked dried out and stale. I didn't buy a slice and she told some other people. Next thing I knew I was on the prayer list for my finances. She can't possibly be on God's list, but she is definitely on mine.

CONTENTS

CHAPTER VIII

APPENDIX

ACKNOWLEDGEMENTS

Thank you Father God for your guidance and every miraculous event you performed before my sight. In a dream I heard your voice instructing me to write and this is the product of your command. I pray for every ear to hear and every eye to see the truth, understanding the meaning and accept You as their Lord and Savior who reads this book. Thank God Almighty for offering us salvation through the acceptance of your Son, Jesus Christ!

Thank you Mom, you are the miracle of my youth and my gift from God.

—Joan C. Lewis—

<u>Special Thanks</u>

Athena Haley
Charles Coleman III
Charlotte Reescano
David J. Lewis
Herbert Ryan Jr.
Kurt Seland

CONTEMNED

by

M. Lewis Ryan

2011

CHAPTER I

It was a long hot summer's day today, in Houston, Texas. The land that God blessed with his own hands seemed to be the vacation spot for Satan and his crew. The temperature kept rising and so did everyone's temper. Driving home is like going on an adventure with all the traffic and road repairs there are around town. More and more people are moving to Houston every day. I know the city isn't fixing all the roads at the same time. It takes them three years, just to complete one, and with all of the layoffs, there are not enough employees to do the necessary repairs.

Why can't anyone find a job these days? I passed five people under the age of twenty seven living beneath the freeway overpasses asking for money at the stop lights today. What is this world coming to that it hasn't reached?

Finally, I've made it home, thank you God. It is a blessing to have a home to come to. There are so many people losing their homes to eviction and foreclosures today more than ever. However, I can't park in my driveway and open my door before the neighborhood crack head comes asking me for money. Who do these people think I am? I won the Range Rover in the divorce, along with the house and everything in it, including the kids. That's what happens when you catch your husband cheating on you. I guess I understand why they think I have something.

Oh, I knew I should have stopped and gotten a pizza. No one has cooked a thing as usual. Well, it is a macaroni and cheese night tonight. I am so tired of grownups not being responsible! Why must I come home every day to a dirty house? Probably because they know that I will clean it again and again.

At least the house is quiet for once. It hasn't been this quiet in a while. I may as well turn on the news. I call it my daily soap opera. It always has something intriguing to see and hear. It has all the elements, murder, theft, drunk drivers, car chases, shoot outs, tornados, hurricanes, floods and fires.

What? No news today. Oh, our President is making yet another speech. These days I can't get away from him and his speeches. They pop up on my computer when I check my email, and I receive emails from him. Before he became President, I didn't even know his name.

I never have thought much about the political scene. All I see is the President making promises, and never delivering positive results. He uses the media to make the public think the way he wants us to think and to see only what he wants us to see. He has more broken promises on his record than my leap year dad. I call my dad leap year because I only heard from him every four years. He would make a promise and never keep it. He must have died. It's been seven years now since I heard from him. I don't think I told him about my kids, his grand kids. I wouldn't have wanted him appearing in their lives only to disappear again, leaving me with all the broken promises that he would never have kept anyway.

Awe! Once again the President is promising jobs. I wish I could afford to live in the dream state where he resides and I am not talking about Washington DC. Pretty soon, there won't be anyone left in the city that will need a job because they are all going to kill one another. There are so many people dying from the heat in their homes because they are too old to live alone and it cost too much for them to move to one of those senior living centers. The young ones are running amuck, they have absolutely no direction and no sense of pride. They will rob you while you're taking out your trash. The only good thing is you have time to shoot them while they are trying to escape because their pants are too low for them to run. There may as well be jeans made with boxers already attached. I wonder if anyone has thought about that as a money maker yet.

It would be nice to have new jobs. If my pay decreases any more from pay cuts, I will be paying the transit center to work. I swear it feels like I should be allowed to claim my job as a dependent. I have been a bus driver for seventeen years and I never remember it being as hard as it is now. The new insurance plan is coming up with some type of monitoring device. They say it's as simple as getting a flu shot. The only bad thing is it leaves a mark like the smallpox vaccine does. It looks like three tear drops kind of in a circle. I don't want it. I hate needles. HR says everyone will have to get it soon for identification. There are so many people stealing identities these days.

I already gave up driving on the holidays because of the law that says if you refuse a breathalyzer the police have the right to take your blood. I know I didn't vote for that so it was obviously squeezed in on me. I wonder what new bill became a law while I slept last night. What's the deal with needles, geez? Yeah that is my real objection, the needles. Why can't they make vaccines in pill form?

God I am tired. I don't know if it's from the heat of the sun or the continuous driving. That bus door opens and closes all day long and the wheels on the bus go round and round. If I hear another kid singing that song I swear I'll commit harry-carry like a Japanese Warrior.

I have too much to do before I go to bed tonight. Today was a full day, but every Monday is a full day in this house. In the morning I thank God for a new morning and for the new chance to live a sin-free life. I pray every day for same thing. It seems like I learn something I thought I already knew each new day. I can't help but wonder where have I been all of my life? I know that sounds crazy, but I also realize I am not the only one who wonders that same thing. I hear preachers talking on television about the end of the world coming. The weather is bad everywhere and there is more and more corruption, confusion and wars than ever before. I go to church and do my best to be a Christian.

I try to make each day sin free and I fall short most days. I cannot make it through driving to work without cursing at someone and then asking for forgiveness. I am usually in a rush and I have absolutely no time for some slow driver. Besides that, my air went out in my car and it is going to cost an arm and a leg to get it fixed. Don't get me started on the price of gas! My alarm sounds at 5:30AM Monday through Friday. I roll out of bed and onto my knees to pray. By the time I am showered and out of the house my morning prayer turns into: Stop riding my ass! Get out of my way! Bright lights, Are you serious!!! Then I have to pray again, because my thoughts for the other drivers on the road are anything but nice and Christ-like. Satan is busy at work on me in a hot car with temperatures close to 100 degrees and a slow ass driver in the front of me. See what I mean, I lose my temper just thinking about them. I want to go to heaven in the rapture. I really want to be one of God's chosen people. It seems like life keeps getting in my way.

My name is Genesis and I live in Houston, Texas, better known as H-Town. I work at Sacred Seniors Adult Day Care part-time to increase my monthly income. I am a Metro Bus Driver full-time. I recently divorced my cheating husband or he divorced me, but who cares about the details. All I know is I am working my behind off to try to stay afloat. Maybe I should have stayed married to his trifling ass. Oops, there I go, Lord forgive me! My blood pressure rises just thinking about the man!

Look at this house. Nothing would ever get done around here without me. The highlight of my day is going out with my girls for our little nightly get together after work.

We go to DJ's Blue Note Café and listen to the poets do their spoken word. My favorites are Liquid Poetry and Eboni Skye. They set that place off talking about some real smooth stuff with the blues playing in the background. It's a classy little joint where professional singles meet. Who knows, I might hit the jackpot and find Mr. Right there tonight. Even Mr. Right Now would be okay for me. It has been too long since I was in a decent relationship with benefits. Those benefits that make your toes curl and send your body on trips of unknown horizons of ecstasy. Yep, that is what I am missing in my life. I am off tomorrow and my daughter is at my mother's house, so I can party tonight as long as I want. Who knows, I might visit a new horizon myself tonight.

I have my rules. I don't mess with married men. Obviously, my ex-best friend did not share my feelings. She had an affair with my husband. I was the last one to find out about it. The church members knew, my friends knew and my family. I guess I really played the fool for at least thirteen of the seventeen years I spent believing in my man and trying to make it work. I only loved him in a godly way and had to learn how to do that, so no sweat off my back. He apologized, but it wasn't the first time he cheated, it would however be the last time for him to cheat on me. If a man can cheat on you with your best friend, you need to let him go.

Since it takes two to tangle, it was just as much her fault as it was his. I wished them happiness together and sent them both packing out of my life. At least I thought it would be that easy, but life is not always fair.

She had been my friend since we were in high school together. She was like my sister because of our closeness. I mean she practically grew up in my house. She said she had a weak moment and that she was going through a lot at time she backstabbed me. Well, she didn't use the words backstab, but it meant the same. I was too occupied with school and marriage, kids plus work to hear what she was going through so she decided to talk to my husband and one thing led to another were her exact words.

It felt like the scene from the Jerry Springer Show was being played in slow motion over and over again in my head. The words just kept repeating and there was no way to block it out of my mind.

We had met for lunch near the Galleria at a little deli as we had many times before and she told me she slept with Bryan. I must be a sheltered dreamer because I actually asked, Bryan who? I say a sheltered dreamer because I romanticize everything from the lack of romance in my life. Not to mention that I would never have even considered she could and would hurt me so badly; especially not her, the person I would have given up my life to protect. Wow, it still hurts. Enough of dwelling on the past cause it just doesn't matter anymore. The funny thing is she didn't even want him. She was just jealous of what she thought I had with him. Really, she was jealous of nothing, but everything happens for a reason. I don't think I know what love is all about. Not the true stuff. I mean those relationships that last for years and years. Are those people insane and can't make it without each other or did they meet their soul mate? Is there really such a thing as a soul mate? I need to stop day dreaming and start cleaning.

How can so many things need to be done in a house of six people and only three of them are kids. My sister and her two kids are living here with me for now and she doesn't have a job. The kids are two and four years old and obviously my responsibility in this house. My sixteen year old son's only responsibilities are attending school, keeping his room clean, playing sports and bugging me about buying him a car. He has two out of four of those down to a tee. And then there is my wonder child. She is my seven year old helpmate when she is not spending the night at my mothers.

Okay, the mac is cooked, the house is organized and that means I am finished with the daily routine. It's party time!

I need to hurry and get dressed because the girls will be here soon. I can hear them complaining already. It is always the same routine. Sandra is the clueless nymphomaniac and Tonya is the down to earth best friend that is hiding from love. Oops, there's the car horn. I have to hurry!

~DJ'S BLUE NOTE CAFÉ~

Monday Night
Features:
Liquid Poetry and Eboni Skye

Why do we always have to be late? There are no seats close to the stage left. Sandra complained about the same thing every week. We arrived right in time to hear Liquid Poetry.

Girl that man melts my heart, said Tonya.

We were all glued to his sleek style. There is nothing like a redbone with black pride, soul and substance. I had been a fan of his for a few years now and kind of followed his artistic life. I guess my inner thought wondered why I couldn't have married someone like him, handsome, educated and reserved. A man, who desires his family, loves his wife and yet shares his love and passion in his art with the world.

Everyone started whistling and then there was complete silence and the lights went dimmer. The bass player and drummer started and that was when Liquid Poetry began to speak:

THE FEATHERS OF MA 'AT

I Heard Her Calling Me Away From The Edge,
As I Leaned Forward Into The Abyss . . .
She Could Have Let Me Fall,
But Saved My Life With A Kiss . . .
I Could Have Surrendered Them All—
The Past Lives I Used To Live.
Too Many Bruises On My Heart—
Not Enough Faith Left To Forgive!
Not Enough Strength Left To Keep On Fighting,
With Fists That Were Made Of Flesh And Bone . . .
At 5 a.m . . . . The Taxi Pulls Way . . .

No One Even Notices That I've Left Home.
No One Notices The New Sun Rising
Over The Deepest Regret Of My Life . . .
For Seven More Years I Still Wore My Wedding Ring
Even Though SHE Was No Longer My Wife!
But The Ultimate Reward Of TRUE Sacrifice
Can Only Be Known By A Crown Of Thorns . . .
Can Only Be Appreciated By Hands That Embrace Nails
And Flesh Allowing Itself To Be Torn . . .
By A Lover Who Loves SO Deeply,
That, In Spite Of His Own Demise,
In Order To Save One Soul,
He Embraces All Of The Lies . . .
He Embraces All Of The Sin,
With Arms Created To Truly Forgive . . .
So I Willingly Surrender THIS Son Of Man,
Knowing HER World Will Live.
But Time Is Relative
In The Shadows Of A Tomb . . .
Where Mortal Flesh Is Devoured,
My Soul Would Not Be Consumed . . .
My Hearts Desire Would Not Be Extinguished,
Before The Sight Of Bridges Burning . . .
Instead My Eyes Embraced The Flames
That Left The Blind And Forever Yearning!
My Lips Embraced The Whispers
Of A Poets Dream, Deferred . . .
But My Prayers were Never Answered—
Maybe They Were Never Heard?
Maybe I Was Never Worthy?
Never Meant To Touch The Son?
Never Meant to Know The Voice
That Called Me HOME To Eden?
Never Meant To Know A Love
That Was So Much Deeper Than My Shame?
I Thought Paradise Was Lost, To Me, Forever,
Until SHE Called My Name!
Until She Took My Pain

And The Sum Of All My Fears . . .
Anointed My Lips With Her Kiss . . .
Washed My Feet With Her Tears . . .
Ignited My Soul With A Passion
That Another Lovers Touch Could Not . . .
Then Weighted My Heart On The Scales
Against The Feathers Of Ma 'at.
She Said, "If You Will Be My King,
Then Baby I Will Be Your Queen.
Together We Can Show These Streets A Love
That They Ain't Never Seen . . .
Together We Can Pierce The Heavens
And Shake The World When We Touch . . .
Then Smile At Our Haters—
Go Ahead, Envy Us!
In God We Trust,
As We Re-Trace The Steps,
That Lead Us Back To Our Beginnings,
In The Garden, Where We Slept . . .
. . . Before The Betrayals And Lies,
When You And I Still Believed . . .
When You Were The Image Of God,
And I Was The Image Of Eve . . ."
She Spoke To Me In The Spirit Words
That Were Written On My Soul.
She Said, "You Are The Missing Piece Of Me,
Only, Together, Can We Be Whole!"
She Knew Why I Had Been Running,
For So Long, To Escape My Past . . .
That We Were Both Children Of Eden,
Duly Judged And Outcast . . .
But That Our Sin Had Been Forgiven,
By One Perfect Sacrifice.
She Said, "I Open Myself To You, Again,
Now Let Me Show You Paradise!"

—LiquidPoetry

Wow, that man knows what a woman wants to hear and what a woman needs to hear. He is so deep! Everyone was knocking and snapping in the club.

Sandra decided she was going to give him her phone number this time and I snatched it out of her hand. "He's married with a newborn son, I said, so back off." I really don't like home wreckers looking for the loose screw in someone's relationship. If they look long and hard enough, they always find it. Even if it was only loose for a moment. He definitely does have a way with words though. By the time he finishes his set, this place is going to be all steamed up! Definitely Sandra will be loose and out of control as usual. People in-love will be snuggled tightly together, singles will start to prowl and the recently separated, divorced or widowed will quietly drop a tear in their glass as they reminisce of past love.

I wished I could feel that way again about a man, but it was a quiet thought that I kept locked deep inside. My ex-husband ruined my trust in the male species. Now, all I hear are a bunch of lying words that I wished were remotely true. Liquid Poetry seems genuine, but they all do at first. It isn't until after you marry them that they change on you. They have all the right words to catch your attention and no substance to make it last. I guess some guys could say the same thing about some women.

Why can't more of the right women and men meet and marry? You know the ones I am speaking of, those who actually know what marriage is all about and have the decency and integrity to make it work. The ones who grow old together and their every word and look is a picture worth taking or a recording you could listen to while sipping fresh coffee on a breezy morning sitting on the dock of the bay.

Here comes my girl, Eboni Skye. I feel her words. They touch me and no one has to know just how much. I can knock and snap with everyone else and inside know that someone understands me. Come on Eboni, I chanted with the crowd and Eboni Skye approached the microphone. There was a sharp bass drum beat preluding her crisp words:

A WOMAN SCORNED

You don't want to hear what I have to say
It's just another day with me in the same ole way
Talking about the same ordeal
The same spill, the same situation causing chills
I am mad tonight
Another day to welcome me into an empty plight
There is no one to yell at about him being unfair
Can't take it out on my kids and he no longer resides here
I should have kept him around until it was out of my system
But his smooth words mixed with wine and this rib can't resist
him
Rib I say simply because woman is the rib of man
One rib for every man I was told was God's plan.
So, he was my Adam and I his Eve
My womb was his truth so with his seed I conceived
Only to find out that I was sharing with another
My husband before God yet he was another woman's lover
His name when spoken was once my soul's release
He was supposed to be the keeper of my love, security and
peace
And I know I loved him and probably still would
But love fueled with anguish is Death with a scythe and black
hood
And why do I feel this way you say
Because he has caused my relations to become torn
And because I
I am a woman scorned
The Reaper has separated my body from my soul
My hands are empty without love to hold
Blind me from truth and allow me to live the lie
Seize this scorned heart causing beauty to die
For years I spoke the words of romance
My head swirled in the bliss of the dance
Until the day my words were stolen
When I became trash, no longer considered golden
When he became my enslaver to doom

Locking my spirit inside of a 4477sq ft. 5 bedroom 3 ½ bath 3
car garage tomb
Which together we obtained through love for all to see
My guess is that several women wanted to be me
Funny thing is how transferrable sex is in the night
Or the smell of sex on your husband arriving home in the
morning light
The sun doesn't shine and yet I live
Chained to my morals, my last breath I give
Forgive me are two words too often used
While I'm left standing lost, dazed and confused
I had to woman up, someone had to appear to be grown
While an invisible third party in my bed had me feeling all
alone
Watching him sleep, a knife appeared in my hand
All the pain and disgust was forming a plan
Trying to do the right thing, I spared his life
Although to death do us part was the agreement as his wife
And why do I feel this way you say
Because he has caused my relations to become torn
And because I
I am a woman scorned
He is paying child support out the zig-zing
And I have left this man without a single thing
And yet my anger still slowly burns
From a simple match it has taken a vital turn
Hell can't contain the consuming flame
I want him buried without a name for the shame
I walked away from my family out of embarrassment
Washed off the stench of another woman's scent
Stood by this father, example to my son
Who asked me why is daddy gone
Six years in and I found an earring in my bed
A gift for me he thought he had lost is what he said
Can't go outside the house without the neighbor shaking her
head
Feeling rather trapped and tight chested wishing I was dead
And why do I feel this way you say

Because he has caused my relations to become torn
And because I
I am a woman scorned
Not sure if this private hell will ever go away
Loss of dignity and pride was the cost I had to pay
Child custody every other weekend drives me insane
Renewing a contemned anguish which is followed by pain
Divorce is a long agonizing death for the living
No love to offer and falsely working on forgiving
And why do I feel this way you say
Because he has caused my relations to become torn
And because I
I am a woman scorned

Eboni Skye

I swear it is as if she lived that part of my life instead of me. She spoke every thought, feeling and emotion I was experiencing, that I am experiencing. A part of me wanted to cry and another part wanted to tell her I understand. She would probably think I was nuts, walking up to her with tears in my eyes saying yes Eboni yes. Where do I go from here is what I would ask her? How do I get my life back and release the anger I fell inside.

She seems so in control of her life while my life is totally out of control. I have a pretty good front going on for my girls, my kids, family, job and the church members. And, no one can say that I was not dignified through my divorce and that it affected me in any way when he moved into my ex-best friend's apartment with her and her kids and left his own kids behind for weekend visits.

The first year we were married, he pushed me down when my leg was broken. By the second year, I was pushing him around out of anger for the first year. Oh Lord, I don't need to think about what happened. I just need to sit here, listen to Eboni and order a drink. Where is the waitress? Waitress!!!

13

I don't remember leaving the club, but my bed never felt so good. I love DJ's Blue Note Café. I could go there just about every night. I usually have a couple glasses of white wine and on hard nights I may have a few more along with a couple shots of Patron. Last night was a hard night.

Who is making that noise? It's too early in the morning for that kind of racket. They need to turn that car alarm off and quiet that dog before it wakes up old lady Smith. She has already threatened to shoot the dog several times. Tonight I could shoot him myself if my world would stop spinning. My stomach wants to relinquish all of its insides.

Oh God, I think I am going to be sick. I will just lay here. Maybe if I put one foot on the floor everything in my head will stop moving. I feel awful. I need my trashcan. I wish I had magical powers to make the trashcan come here to me.

Why am I so awake? Someone must be thinking about me, at least that's what the old people use to say. "I wish they'd stop thinking so I can lie here and just die." What time is it anyway? Where's my cell phone? Oh yeah, it's under my pillow. I keep it there in case of an emergency, that way I won't have to look for it and waste time. Never know when you might have to call the police.

What time does it have on it? 3:00 AM! I didn't fall to sleep until around 1:00AM. No one should have texted me between 1 and 3 in the morning besides my girls with all their same crap. I hope they know that just because they give me a name of the john they are going home with that they don't know anything about, doesn't mean I want to get involved if they come up missing or something worse. I can't bring different men into my house all the time. I have two kids to think about. I just need to get some sleep. Maybe reading a book will put me back to sleep. I know reading my Bible does. My eyes are too tired to read and besides that I really don't feel good.

What is that sound? I think I hear someone in the house. Either someone is in the house or their trying to get into the house. I know heard glass breaking. The neighbors must be fighting. I hear shouting outside. I am not getting involved. When I had my arguments with my Bryan, the last thing I wanted was the neighbors to get involved. The next day they always had that look on their face, that look that says poor pitiful you or the hidden smile of laughter.

No, I hear someone moving around out there. I think someone has broken in to my house. I should call 911. Where's my phone? Where did I put it! I just had it in my hand. Wait! My alarm light is still on. No one has broken into the house, other than the houseguests that forgot their way home.

My sister, Bri, and her two kids moved to Houston about six months ago. It didn't take long before she lost her job and needed a place to stay. I think she is running away from her marriage all together. She won't talk about it without becoming defensive and arguing. We haven't really spoken to each other in a couple of days about anything.

Each morning it seems like a different guy is coming from her room. I told her that has to stop. I am her older sister, but she doesn't listen to me or anyone else. She needs to respect my home and watch what she says and does in front of my two kids. I have tried to instill good lessons and moral principles into them both.

My son's name is BJ, which is short for Bryan Jr., and my daughter's name is JoAnn but we call her JoJo. She was named after her grandmother Joan. They should be in their rooms asleep at this time of night. I forgot that JoJo stayed at moms last night. It has to be BJ. The older BJ gets, the later he stays awake and then he wants to sleep later into the day. I allow him to stay up because it is the summer and he has nothing better to do. At least he is in the house and not running the streets, on drugs and God only knows what else. Surely he would have heard something.

It could be my sister. I don't know what I was thinking to let her and her kids come stay with me? It was supposed to be for a week, then two and now they've been here for months. The fact that she is in my house stays on my mind, repeating itself because I don't want her here. Too much drama comes with Bri. They have got to go. I love her kids, they are my niece and nephew, but damn. They are loud and run all over my house. They already broke my favorite Thomas Blackshear piece and I told them to stay out of my formal living room.

Oh I know what I can do to fall back asleep. I can watch some of my recorded shows I missed. Television helps me to fall asleep. As long as I set the timer everything will be okay. Otherwise, it will wake me out of my sleep when the programs change. Where's Jerry's Program I recorded? This week's topic was: Are You Gay or Not! Let's see, okay there it is. Let me fluff my pillow and get comfy.

Look at that! What is wrong with these people? Girl your boyfriend is really an old woman. How can you not tell? Ut-oh! I didn't see that coming. She decided that your baby brother has turned her back straight and brought you on Jerry to tell you she is a female and that she is leaving you for your 18 year old brother. Wow! Girl you need to yank that wig off her head and whip her butt. No forget all that pulling hair stuff, you need to knock her butt clean out and then get with your brother for a serious talk. Don't believe her, she's not sorry. Watch her kiss your brother when he comes out. Yep! That's what I thought.

I could have swallowed a softball with that yarn, and that was a good stretch. That is enough TV for now, I am going back to sleep for a while. I just want to check my Facebook first. I hope that fine doctor hit me back in my messages. The things I could do with a man like that by my side. Tall, handsome and don't have any kids. I don't know his real name yet, but I call him Butter. He looks smooth like butter. He would make a great father figure for my son. A lot better than what he's got now. Dr. Butter is everything that Bryan is not. Bryan is the average bi-racial blue collar guy. The only thing they have in common is skin tone.

It must have been the hottest Texas summer heat wave of all time for me to marry Bryan. What in the heck was I thinking? I just wasn't ready for marriage. I should have stayed in college and sent my baby home to my mom's house. But, no. Not me. I didn't want to be embarrassed, so I optioned marriage at the age of eighteen years old. I had only been in college for a short time when I found that one fraternity party. I wish I had never gone. I should have listened to my mother's advice and stuck to my lessons. But no, I had to do things my way.

My mother had struggled for a long time to send me to college and offer me a decent life. She taught us that we were queens and should be respected as royalty. She said every woman should respect and carry herself in that manner, and if a man did not treat us as such, we should get away as fast as possible.

I guess I didn't understand what she was saying when I was younger. I understand perfectly now. I wish I had waited before acting like a common whore, instead of the royalty she raised. How could I have disappointed her that way? Through it all she never criticized me. She prayed for me and helped me in every way she could. That's why I named JoJo after her. I hope she turns out to be the daughter that my mother deserves, because God knows I'm not.

I am thinking about too much crap. I am just going to lay here and close my eyes. It's probably Dr. Butter thinking about my body. I bet he is long and hard in thought, looking at those pictures of me in leather and lace I sent him. Thank God for the internet. Oh yeah, with the thought of Dr. Butter on my mind, I can definitely fall asleep.

The clock says 9:00AM. I need to get up! Oh God, I still feel like crap, but I think there is a sale at the mall today. Is today Tuesday? Yes it is and the sale starts at eleven. So, that gives me two hours to get there. I should be ready by ten. All I have to do is call up my girls so we can roll out.

No signal on the phone again, I am so tired of this phone. I bought it because it's supposed to never lose signal and it is a piece of junk. All of that money for a phone that is either busy or there is no signal. I guess I have more of a signal with this service than the other carriers. I will just use the house phone.

I need some coffee to start this day. Actually, I need coffee to start every day. Oh great! Bri is sitting in the living room and looking high as hell. I am so tired of this, but I promised mama to let her stay with me. I didn't promise she could stay for this long, but I guess that doesn't matter because she's family.

I may as well start the sarcasm. One of us is going to do it, so I may as well be first.

Good morning Brianna. Good morning Brianna! What's wrong with you? Why are you sitting in the living room like you lost your best friend? Bri, do you hear me talking to you? What's up with you? Are you still not talking to me? Listen, you live in my house!

I was ready for the showdown. I knew it had been coming. She had gotten on my last nerve and by now I knew I was on her last nerve too. Sisters know each other all too well and we also know each other's limits. I don't know why we argue so much. I love my sister and she knows that I do, but that knowledge never has stopped us from getting into the biggest fights with one another. Bri stood up and came towards me. I grab the closest weapon to me, which was my son's baseball. She looked at me, shook her head and said, "Drop the ball and listen". Next, she screamed at me.

Shut up and listen to me! My kids are gone. Did you hear me? My kids are gone!

What? I replied, placing the baseball down on the counter. Gone where? Did your husband take them? I told you to straighten everything out with him before you took his kids away from Chicago. You were the one who made a mess of your relationship.

You were the one who had a baby for another man and got caught. You were the one having sex with the nanny, not him.

Bri screamed at me again, shut up!!! I called and spoke to him and his mother last night and we reached an understanding.

What type of understanding? What could you possibly say to a man who has caught you in more situations than a little bit. A man who actually forgave you each time and that you left in the middle of the night taking his kids with you. There is no understanding that!

It doesn't matter right now Genesis. My kids are gone. I woke up this morning, and their beds were empty. Where are they? I was home all night. Where are they?

I was at a loss for words. My mind went blank. Are you saying that someone broke into the house and took the kids? I knew I had heard something around 3:00AM.

Where is your homeboy from last night? Didn't he stay with you? I told you about bringing different people into my house. Have you called the police yet?

Bri held up her cell phone and said, "It has been busy all morning. I can't get a signal. Will you take me to the police station?"

"Why can't you drive yourself", I asked?

The battery is dead in my car. Nothing seems to be working right this morning. Oh, by the way, his name is Mark and he is in the bathroom and I would appreciate you watching what you say around him. He might be the one.

They are all the right ones according to you for at least a week. You are a married woman Bri. You need to exhibit a little more respect for yourself.

Oh you mean like mom did by allowing daddy to walk all over her, while she tried to play ignorant of the fact that he was the biggest whore in town. I am not like mom. I don't take that kind of mess off of no man.

No you don't. Instead, you decided to become the whore.

"I guess I am just like daddy", exclaimed Bri.

I guess you are. Are you sure you didn't abandon your kids at moms since you are so much like him. Stop! Let's not do this right now. Check with mom and see if she has the kids and if she doesn't I will drive you to the police station.

Bri had been out drinking with Mark the night before, and yes, she gets in early, but that is because she is too drunk not too. Nothing is ever working right when you are drunk. I wanted to tell her that she was drinking too much, but she was already paranoid about the kids, so I figured I would let it slide for now. She wasn't exactly rational this morning. What the hell is she talking about now?

She was blabbering, "What if all the kids are gone? Then what? It's like that movie where the kids come up missing and my kids are gone! Then she ran to the window, yanked the curtains open and said what if everyone is gone!"

Finally I had to put a stop to her madness. I went outside and came back in to report. There isn't anyone gone. Everybody is outside as usual. Debo, the local crack head, was still hustling money, old lady Smith is still yelling at the neighbor's dog and Mr. Jones just winked at me while he was taking out his trash. Outside has the same ole people, doing the same ole things.

Bri laughed for a moment and then she started to cry. She turned with a serious stone look on her face and asked me, "Where are your kids?" I could see Bri was about a moment from snapping.

They had better be upstairs cleaning their rooms like I told them to do yesterday. I turned and looked towards the upstairs and yelled, BJ and JoAnn, come down here right now! I had just located my keys when I heard BJ's voice.

What mama?

Boy, don't what mama me! Where is JoJo? He looked in his pockets and around his back and finally said, "I guess she stayed at mema's last night. That's where she's usually at every day."

Did she take your little cousins with her? He quickly replied, "mama who do I look like? Why would I know?"

He had outgrown me in height and for sixteen he stood at 6'4". I still could have snatched him into next week for his attitude. My blood boiled quickly and before I knew it, I was yelling at him.

Get out of my sight! You sound just like your daddy! I swear you act more and more like him every day. Just because you are sixteen, don't think you are grown. If I didn't need the child support, I would send you to live with your damn daddy. He walked back to his room and I could hear the door slam. He always showed his butt when he returned from his dads' apartment. It usually takes him a couple of days to snap back to reality.

I had just picked him and his sister up from their dads Sunday after church. He still had another day of grace before attitude adjustments would be necessary. JoJo was never a problem. At times I wondered if they switched her in the hospital and someone else is raising my hell raiser. I told Bri, "Let's cover all of our bases before going to the police."

Bri, you need to walk over to moms if you cannot reach her by phone. I bet she has your kids over at her house. You know mama. She always let them come over as soon as they ask her, whether they asked us or not. She has always been that way. Always preaching to them about the bible, I am surprised they even want to go to her house at all. When you get there, tell JoJo I said to bring her behind home too.

Bri thought about it for a moment in her delusional state and agreed to walk to mama's house. She only lived a couple of blocks away. "You're right", she said, "I am going to walk over there now." I was hoping that the walk would actually be a calming experience for her. I made sure to tell her to take her overnight guest with her and to not bring him back. I should have start charging room and board on night two of that mess.

BJ, come go to the store for me, the one around the corner and nowhere else. He loved driving the car anywhere. He would always take the long routes to show his friends that he was driving. I needed him to buy me some aspirins for my own vicious hangover. He flew down the stairs, grabbed the keys and was out of the door in a flash. I just laughed at him when he walked back in to find out what I wanted from the store.

Finally, I get a moment of peace. Let me go say my morning prayer to God. I know I need to pray after the dream I had of Dr. Butter last night. Today is going to be a good day. I'm thinking that we should try that new mall out. I bet they still have some grand opening sales going on. God if you will let me find a killer purse and sunglasses to go with my new pumps that will definitely make my day. Oh yeah, and don't let me curse no one out at the mall. Thank you and Amen.

Bri came rushing back inside of the house in a panic. Just then BJ ran in crying and shaking. They were both screaming at the top of their lungs. They kept pacing the floor, back and forth. I thought my heart was going to explode from watching them.

What's wrong? I knew it had to be something serious. BJ was not the type of kid who was easily shaken. They were making me nervous! "What's wrong", I asked again?

Finally, Bri caught me by the shoulders and glared into my eyes. "It's happened", she said.

My mind began to spin. What was she talking about? What has happened? "What", I asked? What's happened?

The rapture happened! They are gone, all of them, gone! Some old man on the street was saying that we are all going to hell because we missed the rapture!

BJ ran up to me and started screaming. "Why were we left here, mom? Why? There is an airplane in the middle of the block on the next street over. Cars and trucks are everywhere with no one in them. Why mom", he cried.

Just then, Bri said, "Mom is gone! Mom, JoJo, and my kids are gone." She sat on the floor and an uncontrollable shaking took over her body and she wept.

All of a sudden I thought, that means the sale is probably not going to happen today. Where was my mind? Was I in shock? How can this be? I was just like everyone else. I partied on Monday Night and sometimes, but not often on Friday and maybe Saturday Night, but every Sunday I was in church. I never missed church. I even sang in the choir. The more I thought, the angrier I became. How could God have been so blind that he didn't see me at church? I didn't live my life any different than any other Christian in that church. Then it hit me. I hadn't missed the rapture. This was just another crazy person saying the rapture was coming. Wait! Those crazies say it is coming, not that it has happened!

I may have forgotten to pray last night but I prayed this morning. What is really going on? There is no way I missed the rapture. Anyway, everyone is supposed to see Jesus return to Earth. The bible says so. I didn't see Jesus last night! I didn't see any dead people walking around on the streets, and that is supposed to happen also. No, the rapture had not happened. I wouldn't be here still. Something else is going on today. Maybe Satan has caused people to disappear or something. Maybe there was a bomb like 9-11 and it caused the plane to crash. I heard sirens, but we hear sirens all the time. There is always something happening. We already live in hell daily, so the rapture probably already happened years ago. Mom probably took the kids shopping or something. My heart began to beat harder as I tried to make sense of what these maniacs were saying to me. I have heard some preachers say that the rapture is at the end of the world and we would not be alive if it was the end of the world. I DID NOT MISS THE RAPTURE!!!

An announcement broadcast appeared on the television. It said the world had been attacked by aliens and a large number of people were abducted. The President came on with an emergency message: Do not panic. The government has everything under control. We have dispatched spaceships out to locate our family members and friends in order to return them home safely. For a moment, I almost cheered, until reason set in to my delusional state. I tried desperately to grab ahold of what the President was saying and make it make sense, but something didn't feel right.

I knew that what he was saying was a lie. Spaceships and aliens coming to Earth to take the children and my mother didn't sound logical. My mother did not raise a fool. I needed to know who was missing. I needed to see if all the Christians I knew were gone. I knew the truth. If they are gone, then the rapture had come and I had been left behind. I ran for my Bible and quickly turned to Revelation.

I had not read the Bible on my own in a while. I would flip through pages at church and I would intend to read it at home later, but I would fall asleep. I wanted to know what to do after the rapture. I knew there would be a second chance to be saved or something like that. I remembered mom saying something about a thousand years and Jesus returning and judgment. Oh God my head hurts! Spaceships, rapture, this is too much for me to deal with right now!

"BJ, sit down and stop pacing the floor", I yelled!

"What are we going to do now", he asked? Bri looked at me waiting for an answer. The person, who never listened to me, now expects me to guide us out of this mess. I had nothing. I did not know what to do or where to start. I wanted to cry, scream, run and shout. I wanted to know why? Why did he leave me? Why did he leave my son? I wanted my mother! I was fighting back the hugest urge to cry I ever had. I choked down so many tears till I could barely speak from the pain in my throat.

BJ looked at the TV. He jumped up and said the President is looking for volunteers to clean up the city streets. "I am going to help! I am going to go and volunteer", he said.

NO! NO!! NO!!! I think my soul screamed no! I didn't know what to do, but I knew that BJ leaving the house to volunteer was not it. Anyone leaving the house or separating was not the answer. I didn't know Mark very well, but I was glad that a man was in the house with us.

"We need to read the Bible", I said. Bri said okay, but BJ was too bitter. He jumped up again and said he could not sit around and do nothing. He said he was going to help the President get them back.

"Back from where", I yelled! Back from the aliens? "Get real Bryan". You are smarter than that. You know there were no aliens. Look at who's gone. You asked me, why we were left behind. We were left behind because we were not doing the will of God. I thought I was doing his will, but I obviously wasn't and I wasn't being the best example for you.

"Come on Bryan, think! What secrets are you holding on to? What have you been doing that is a sin? You are over the age of twelve, so you are considered a man in the eyes of God. What have you been doing? God doesn't make mistakes", I said as my body collapsed into a sitting position on the floor.

BJ took a deep sigh and dropped his eyes. His voice cracked into sobs. He told of how he and his friends had been smoking marijuana at some guy's house that he didn't know well. He said the other guy was older and he had a girlfriend. The guy said that she wouldn't mind if everyone had sex with her. BJ sobbed harder. "I didn't want to do it", he said. But everyone started calling me names. They said, "I was a fruit and that maybe I was gay." So, I did it! "I did it", he exclaimed! She was bleeding, but I didn't care because I didn't want them to think I was a fruit. I didn't want them to think I was gay! But then, no one else did it, just me. Then, everyone laughed and said I was a real man. The older guy said thanks for breaking that in for him and that he wouldn't tell her who it was. She had taken something and was drunk.

He just wanted to take her virginity away so he could have sex with her whenever he wanted. Her parents tested her and him and found out that she wasn't pregnant and that he hadn't raped her. He gave samples of his DNA and he seemed like the hero who rescued her, when really he set it all up. I felt awful mom! I couldn't say anything! You understand right mom! I, I couldn't say anything. Do you think God hates me now? Is that why he left me here? He was broken and on his knees crying.

I couldn't believe my ears. My son wouldn't do that. The words were coming out of his mouth and I could see him talking, but I couldn't believe what I was hearing. Not my son! My body and soul were without each other. My soul hugged my son and yet my body remained frozen, just looking at him. Tears rolled down my face as I wanted so badly to be that mother, but all I could manage was to remind myself to just breathe. My world was crashing all around me. My son was breaking before my eyes and I did not have the strength to rebuild him. But, my sister, my wonderful confused, beautiful baby sister, took control of the situation.

Bri stood up and walked to BJ. She opened her arms and hugged him. She said everything was going to be alright. Then she looked at me and signaled for me to come over, but my legs remained frozen. I still could not move. I couldn't speak. What he had done was not okay and everything was not going to be alright. All I could think was that we needed to pray. Momma always said that kids do not come with how to books. Then another panic set in. my mother is gone. Oh God! I thought I was I could get through this, but not without her help! Oh God, grief, panic, stress and loss is setting in all at once. I can't handle this. This is too much! And now, my son, sister and I could be going to hell. My head started spinning faster and faster. I no longer had a hangover. I was just sick and becoming deathly ill by the second. I couldn't breathe, my stomach felt awful and my head hurt so bad. I wanted my mother's lap.

Finally I spoke. Words came screaming out of my mouth! "I am going to burn in hells fire for eternity. Oh God help us! Come back and get us Lord! Please God please. I am so sorry for everything I have ever done wrong. Please don't leave me here. Please God please! If I could have torn the skin from my bones I would have. I screamed myself into a complete fit. All my life I had thought my lows were the lowest I could get and feel. No one told me there was a depth that left you with no feelings, no voice, no sense of smell or ability to hear sound. I had experienced heartbreaks and lost loves before, but nothing like this. I had given birth twice, one by natural childbirth, but no pain compared to this. Why was my heart beating? My eyes had seen more than my heart could bear by the time I was 23 years old and now I get the unwanted pleasure of living after the rapture with just enough knowledge to know I am going to hell. "Are you serious God? Well, I guess you were serious all along and it just took me too long to realize just how serious you are."

The doorbell rang twice before I opened the door. I barely had strength to turn the knob. Maybe I thought it was God coming back for me, but it wasn't. It was my ex-husband Bryan Sr. He was standing there with his new bimbo. I opened the door and he rushed inside. He was worried about his kids being abducted by aliens. I had no fight left in me, no smart comebacks and no words at all. The funny thing is it didn't surprise me one bit that he thought aliens had come to Earth, but then again it sounded about right coming from a true sinner. I despised the ground he walked on. Surprisingly enough, no aliens took him or his Bimbo Barbie. Now I knew I was in hell.

He said that people were rioting in the streets and taking everything that wasn't nailed down. BJ ran into the room and threw his arms around his dad's neck. Crying he said, "JoJo is gone dad!"

Bryan turned and looked at me and asked, "How could you let this happen? How could you have been so careless with my daughter?" He questioned my whereabouts last night when he already knew that last night was my night out with the girls. "This is the reason why I want BJ to come live with me", he yelled!

My contempt for this man has to be the reason I missed the rapture. I know I've murdered him a thousand times in my mind. Bimbo Barbie looked at me and said, "I hope you realize we are not paying child support until they find her". Who in the hell was she talking to? Bimbo Barbie's don't talk! I felt my fist clenching. I saw myself slapping this woman into yesterday so she could find a clue and bring it back with her today. Just when I started to ask her who the hell she thought she was talking to, an uncontrollably feeling of laughter came over my body.

"Until who finds her", I asked? I knew what she was going to say, but just had to see how stupid she looked saying it.

She actually replied, "The President's Spaceships". It was times like this that I could see myself going to hell. How dare this bimbo's audacity to stand up in my house and say anything. She isn't even a real person, just the latest screw for the dipshit I made the mistake in marrying. It's bad enough to have to take crap from him, but I refuse to have to deal with this bimbo and him. Since the divorce I have been taking Citalopram Hydrobromide for stress and depression and although my doctor suggested counseling, I just have not had the time to go in for therapy. I prayed to be rescued from this horrible situation, and yet, I was left behind. Imagine that!

What was there to keep me from beating this bimbo like she stole something? Actually, she did, they both did. They stole my chance to go to heaven. I was smoking mad. I wanted to grab them, tie them together and blow both of their brains out of their heads. The more I thought, the angrier I became. Do it! I heard something tell me. Do it, I heard it again. I turned around and around. No one was near me. I hadn't said anything out loud. God wouldn't tell me to do that! I ran to my room and locked the door.

I couldn't escape it. It was with me in my room. "I am losing my mind", I thought. There was a raging fire within me that could not be doused by water. I fell to my knees and began to pray.

Dear God hear my plea
I know you are busy with your chosen
Father please remember me
Hear my voice as I cry out
About nights ruled by the evil son
Now my heart has no doubt
Now that your rapture is done
Oh my God, whom I knew not
Hear my plea to thee
I know now that your son did come
And shed his precious blood for me
Lead my path I pray to you
Douse the evil within
For I am found without a clue
How do I escape my sin?
Anger, jealousy, a wrath
Which burns out of control
Father do what must be done
Please Father save my soul.

Amen

CHAPTER II

Bryan Sr. stepped out the front door. He looked up to the sky and started talking. Why am I still here? Why did you take my little girl and not me? I know she is scared. Don't worry JoJo! Somehow, I am going to get you back here with me. I should have come and taken you away with me after the lesbian moved in. Yeah, she might have two kids and sleep with men now, but once a dike always a dike.

He walked further away from the front door alongside of the house. "I have really made a mess of things", he said, lowering his head and falling down on his knees. He placed his head in his hands and began to sob. Genesis watched him from her bedroom window. She was startled seeing him on his knees and wanted to hear what he was saying. She listened as he pled his case to the sky.

I have lost my daughter and my ex-wife has accused me of doing things that I have not done. I never told anyone I was going to divorce her and marry them. At least not that I remember. During sex doesn't count. I am a man and a real man says whatever needs to be said to get what he wants when it comes to sex. So, no, during sex doesn't count. Yeah, I moved in with her friend after one mistake, but I didn't have any place else to go. Why can't she see and understand that? I gave my life up because of her mistake. I wasn't ready to get married. I took her as my wife, pregnant and all. I wasn't in love with her, I barely knew her. She was my brother's mistake. She owes me. I don't owe her nothing. I am paying child support and she loses my daughter. I hate her and everything she stands for. If it wasn't for me, she would be just like all the other, non-educated, ghetto fabulous with bastard kids, church going, God praising, Jesus freak with a drug habit, asking some invisible

30

God to upgrade her to a double-wide someday. I saved her from all of that and she put me out. Now she is starting to date other men in front of my beautiful children. This is not happening!

She has moved on with her life and I am trying to do the same. Bambi is a wonderful woman and she is willing to help me raise my kids. Is it wrong for me to want my kids to come live with me? Genesis let JoJo be taken away because of her negligence. I will not lose my son too.

Genesis wondered who he was lying to in the sky. Had he become a Christian? It didn't take long for her to realize he was talking to the alleged aliens who had supposedly taken the missing people from earth. Does this man believe the lies he is telling himself. Has he forgotten I was there living through all of the drama. She continued to listen until he disappeared from her sight and range of sound.

He re-entered the house and firmly told BJ to gather his belongings in order to come live with him. We will find your sister and live together as a family. If I had been with JoJo, she would still be here with us. So go head son and get your things.

BJ immediately shouted, "No!"

Your mom is not equipped to take care of you and protect you. Where is she? I will tell you where. She has locked herself inside of her bedroom. I will not leave you here with someone so unstable. And, her sister is not the type of person I want you around. If someone is going to tell you about dating girls, I would rather it be me than your so called aunt.

BJ looked at his dad and told him that was more of a reason for him to stay with his mom. I have to take care of her dad. You have Miss. Bambi, but mom only has me now. Besides, Aunt Bri is good to me dad and both of her kids are gone. Don't you care? Maybe, you should go now. I need to check on mom.

"Come on Bambi!" We have things to do and some places to go. He looked at BJ and told him that he still expected to see him the coming weekend. Make sure you are ready by five o'clock on Friday BJ.

He had made some decisions earlier that week. He planned on getting custody of his children. He had already hired a lawyer to prepare the paperwork. The lawyer told him the best situation would be for him to be married. Bryan smiled at his lawyer and said, "If it is at all possible for me to take the kids from her, I am willing to do anything." Without missing a beat, he turned and asked Bambi to marry him and she agreed.

BJ held no knowledge of his fathers plans. At that moment, he simply wanted his father to leave the house so he could check on his mother's state. He turned to his father and told him quietly, "I will be ready as usual dad." He walked them to the door and said, "Bye, I will see you Friday."

When Bryan Sr. left Genesis house that morning, he and Bambi went straight to the courthouse and got married. Next, they went to see his lawyer and told him about JoJo's abduction. His lawyer then devised a plan for Bryan to gain custody of BJ. He told him to bring BJ to his house and he would have him sign a change of residence which would allow him to submit an immediate temporary custody order. Bryan agreed to the plan of kidnapping BJ. There were so many people being reported as missing till they both knew they could get away with it. After the lawyer's office, they went to get vaccinated. He wanted to ensure that he was safe and that aliens would not be able to take him away. He did not truly understand the devastation of his actions. He talked to God but did not know God nor God's word.

Signs were appearing all over the city, a triangle with an eye in the middle of it and a 6 outside of each angle. Those signs were on bulletin boards as a new development company being announced. Some gas stations and grocery stores were already bearing this emblem. Big Brother was watching and Bryan couldn't see it.

People were committing suicide every time someone would claim the rapture had occurred. This time, there were a lot of suicides. America had become a Third-World country over night. Not really, for those without a clue. They simply blew in whichever direction the wind moved day by day. Bryan was one of the many leaves.

Bryan would attend church once or twice a month with his family, but usually he was busy working. When he wasn't working he was gone for weekend excursions fishing or hunting with colleagues discussing business. Church for Bryan was about social status. He would write his check for tithing and be ready to leave when everyone was praying with their eyes closed. A big televised church with many suits and business connections was his only concern, along with beating the traffic on the way out. After the divorce, he stopped attending church altogether. Genesis and the kids had always been members at the church her mother attended. It was a small nondenominational church with about 50 members. While she and Bryan were married, she would spend at least one Sunday a month going to some big name brand church.

She hated going to the big churches. "They are worse than malls", said Genesis. You can buy books, clothing, backpacks and all kinds of things at church. Jesus even got mad about that! They don't have preachers, they have inspirational leaders. Every time she went with him she would feel lost and out of place. It felt like they had gone to a concert and bought souvenirs for the kids.

Bryan was a mediocre insurance salesman for a major company. He was supposed to be a doctor. His adoptive family paid his way through college and medical school for taking the blame for something that was neither his fault nor his responsibility. Although he was asked to do the deed, he was also disowned and paid off for completing the task. The task in question was to admit to getting Genesis pregnant and marrying her before the baby came. The only child they had together was JoJo, his daughter. BJ was never told the truth about Bryan not being his biological father. Bryan had been in BJ's life from day one, so as far as Bryan was concerned, BJ was always going to be his son.

The rest of the week past by swiftly and Friday had come. A curfew had been placed on the city and after a while, people began to forget about their missing relatives and friends or the ones left here, just did not care. The news only reflected the betterment of society with Big Brother Company coming. Three people had been shot and killed near Genesis house just last night for being out of their homes after dark. It was never mentioned on any of the television channels. There was talk of the Pope touring the world to help bring nations together and help Christians in remorse for their missing loved ones. It felt as if he was endorsing a candidate for a political office. He mentioned one religion, one leader and one law. He spoke of peace and we could all use some peace of mind. He spoke highly of God and reassured everyone that the raptured had not taken place. How could it have taken place when he was still alive and on Earth?

An emergency broadcast announcement came over the radio. It said that some of the people who were taken by aliens had been located and are being kept in quarantine. However, it has been discovered that alien entities are possessing their bodies and that top scientists from around the world are working on a solution to this problem. The President has declared the vaccination mandatory for every human being on earth.

Why does this sound familiar? I know I have never heard this before, a mandatory mark for identity reasons. Wait a minute! Those three tear drops aren't tear drops at all. It is the number 666. It is the sign of the beast, the antichrist. It has started! Oh please someone pinch me and wake me up from this nightmare! Things were bad before the rapture. Food prices were very high and gasoline was almost unaffordable. The Earth was preparing for a major eclipse on December 21, 2012, our year. Now that the true Christians are gone, all hell is breaking loose at a rapid pace. When Earth aligns with the sun and the Milky Way, which is our galaxy, the sun will burn a third of the Earth to total destruction. Wherever daylight is for that alignment is where I don't want to be. Birds and other animals will infest the other portions of the world. Pastor mentioned all of this in Bible Study once. I need to find those scriptures. I know this stuff. Where is my Bible?

Food is getting scarce and Bri is getting weak. We pray every day, but she says that God has the ones he wants and that he can't hear us. I ignore her when she starts talking like that. I know it is not easy for her to give up drinking and smoking and taking pills. She seems to be doing pretty good. She thinks that her kids are being held by the President. She is staying sober for the day she can go pick them up. If he does call, it will be a successful clone of her kids and that's all. Either way, I wonder how long we are going to be able to stay here. My boss is saying that anyone who does not get vaccinated might be laid off for safety and security reasons.

I have saved a little money, but it doesn't really matter much because it is becoming obsolete. Everything is bought with some form of credit that is obtained through the vaccination mark, 666. Gold still works pretty well as a bribe for some. I don't know what to do. I pray every day now, all the time. I don't speak without checking with God first. BJ is a growing boy, he is going to have to eat and then there is Bri, what do I do about Bri.

I hadn't thought about going to church, because I assumed it was taken too. I felt so alone and yet I still wanted to get away from everyone for a while. I told Bri and BJ to stay in the house, but they insisted on coming with me. The church was still there and there were cars parked outside the building. We went inside slowly, not knowing what or who we would find there. I recognized some of the faces. I wasn't happy to see them and yet I was all at the same time. The moment was very bitter sweet. I asked if anyone had seen the pastor and Ricky said they were taken in the rapture. The pastors entire family went, even Sister Anna Mae. I thought about Sister Anna Mae's singing and decided that maybe it isn't about how well you sing a song. Maybe it is about for whom and why you sing the song. If I could just go back to the Sunday I sung my solo. If I had understood what Pastor was talking about instead of how he looked saying it. Oh God Help Me! I have totally lost my mind.

The people in the church were talking about leaving the city. I started thinking about Harriet Tubman. Someone said we need a Moses. BJ walked forward and said, "We have Jesus." He left us with the plans to get to heaven. I couldn't believe my ears. I guess JoJo wasn't the only one listening to mama. He continued saying, "We have the Bible and I don't know about any of you, but it means more to me than food right now. I want to see my baby sister and Mema. Nothing has gone right since they've been gone." Everyone agreed. I took him my Bible and asked him to read to us.

BJ opened the Bible and began to read Hebrew Chapter 13.

1 Let brotherly love <u>continue</u>. 2 Be not forgetful to <u>entertain</u> strangers: for thereby some have entertained angels unawares. 3 Remember them that are in bonds, as bound with them; and them which suffer adversity, as being yourselves also in the body. 4 Marriage is honorable in all, and the bed undefiled: but whoremongers and adulterers God will <u>judge</u>. 5 Let your <u>conversation</u> be without <u>covetousness</u>; and be content with such things as ye have: for he hath said, I will never leave thee, nor forsake thee. 6 So that we may boldly say, The Lord is my helper, and I will not fear what man shall do unto me. 7 Remember them which have the rule over you, who have spoken unto you the word of God: whose faith follow, considering the end of their <u>conversation</u>. 8 <u>Jesus</u> <u>Christ</u> the same yesterday, and today, and forever. 9 Be not carried about with divers and strange doctrines. For it is a good thing that the heart be established with <u>grace</u>; not with meats, which have not profited them that have been occupied therein. 10 We have an <u>altar</u>, whereof they have no right to eat which serve the <u>tabernacle</u>. 11 For the bodies of those beasts, whose <u>blood</u> is brought into the <u>sanctuary</u> by the high <u>priest</u> for <u>sin</u>, are burned without the <u>camp</u>. 12 Wherefore <u>Jesus</u> also, that he might sanctify the people with his own <u>blood</u>, suffered without the <u>gate</u>. 13 Let us go forth therefore unto him without the <u>camp</u>, bearing his reproach. 14 For here have we no continuing city, but we seek one to come. 15 By him therefore let us offer the <u>sacrifice</u> of praise to God continually, that is, the <u>fruit</u> of our lips giving thanks to his name. 16 But to do good and to communicate forget not: for *with such sacrifices God is well pleased. 17 Obey them that have the rule over you, and submit yourselves: for they <u>watch</u> for your souls, as they that must give <u>account</u>, that they may do it with joy, and not with grief: for that is unprofitable for you. 18 Pray for us: for we trust we have a good <u>conscience</u>, in all things willing to live honestly. 19 But I beseech you the rather to do this, that I may be restored to you the sooner. 20 Now the God of peace, that brought again from the dead our Lord <u>Jesus</u>, that great <u>shepherd</u> of the <u>sheep</u>, through the <u>blood</u> of the <u>everlasting</u> <u>covenant</u>, 21 Make you perfect in every good work to do his will, working in you that which is well pleasing in his sight, through <u>Jesus</u> <u>Christ</u>; to whom be <u>glory</u> forever and ever. <u>Amen</u>.*

He did not attempt to explain that which he read. Everyone surrounded him as he stood there with the Bible in his hand. A sixteen year old boy was leading the way. He confessed to the church the reason he believed he was left behind. He asked for their forgiveness and forgiveness from God. And just like that, he became their leader as I watched. They no longer felt the need to run and hide. They forgave and comforted him. It made me wonder just what they had done to be left behind. I hadn't done anything as harsh as these sinners.

I had been the same, the responsible one who gave up her life to care for her kids. I was the one who got married and did the right thing. I was the one who was raped and robbed of her existence. How could he possibly stand there and ask for forgiveness. How dare those hypocrites forgive him? I felt ashamed. I turned and headed out of the church. I could no longer breathe inside of the walls of the church. Once again, my heart was full of malice. Only this time, it was towards my son, not his dad. How could he have done the same thing his dad did. The only difference was that I did get pregnant.

Am I supposed to believe that just like that he has been called into the ministry after what he has done? How could God forgive him, what about the girl's life he has ruined? I hated myself for feeling this way. He is my son, what is wrong with me?

Ricky came outside to find me. I was sitting with my back against the building and my head on my knees. He said, "Let it go". I looked up at him and wondered who are you to tell me anything? He looked me in my eyes and said, "Genesis, Gen, let it go. Whatever it is, let it go". He obviously did not know what it felt like to make something out of nothing, to push and aid a man into becoming someone, while you watch as the life is sucked out of you in every aspect. He did not know what it felt like to be told that this very same man had sex with your best friend in your bed.

He definitely did not know that I did all of this with and for the man who supposedly raped me and got me pregnant and then asked to marry me. I don't remember a lot about that night, but I do remember his brother the superstar basketball player. How could I forget him, he was every girl's dream. He was the one who led me upstairs after spiking my drink. He was the one who wouldn't stop. The next day before I had decided to go to the police or not, Bryan came and asked me to be his girlfriend. He said that he was sorry about what happened to me and that if I was pregnant, that he wanted to marry me. He took all the blame, but I was pretty sure it wasn't him. It was his brother.

I didn't want anyone to know what happened and neither did he and his family. It had been videotaped and his parents saw the tape before either of them woke up the next day. A few weeks later, after my period didn't come, his parents became very busy planning a wedding. I despised my husband and his family.

Over the years I developed an appreciation for him and maybe a love. It went away when I found out he slept with my best friend and now, he has Bimbo Barbie. Not to mention, certain people were all too eager to share their knowledge that he may have cheated another time or two and just didn't get caught.

How do I let it go when it has been a part of me since I was eighteen years old? Why should I let it go? He needs to be punished for what he did to me. I cried out of anger and desperation. I was being punished when it should have been him, them.

I looked at Ricky and said, "I guess we won't be singing today." He smiled at me and said, "We should rejoin the others inside of the church girlfriend." I couldn't help but smile. I knew Ricky meant well. He was probably the only man around that I trusted a hundred percent. Probably because he seemed to be more female than male, if you know what I mean.

I walked inside of the church and straight to BJ and hugged him. I complemented his reading and asked if he wanted to do it again next week. BJ answered quickly and said that he had already agreed to restart the church services. I couldn't help but wonder, "Who is this kid?"

We shuffled around from church to church building. There was mentioning of raids on churches, so we tried to move around as much as possible. We were having service every day since most of the members were living in the church. We had just returned to Love Life Center when the doors to the church flew open and Angela walked inside. She looked around at everyone there and said, "All of you thought you were so much better than me, didn't you? And look at you! You're all here looking pathetic. How many of you are running out of food and money? You use to laugh at me for being on government care. Poor uneducated Angela! Well guess who's laughing now. The government is taking care of me, even without my kids. My kids are doing fine too. They are back from outer space and the President has them in quarantine."

I hadn't seen Angela since the Sunday she came to church wearing the clothes she had on from the night before. She had always been quiet and mousey, but now she was loud and outspoken. People were changing a lot these days. I didn't see when Bri stood up and started talking to Angela.

Bri, all you have to do to see your kids, is go to the base where they are being kept. Take a picture of them so they can locate them for you. As long as you have had your vaccination, you can see your kids. I saw mine and they will be home soon.

Bri asked Angela if the vaccination hurt at all. Angela answered, "No more than any other shot." She said, "But afterwards, you feel like you own the world." That was all Bri needed to hear, she had wanted an escape and now there was a legal way to get the feeling of being high. Besides that, she gets to see her kids.

"Where do I go to get the vaccination", Bri asked? I grab Angela's hand and held it out. I told Bri to look. The number 666 in a circular form was on her hand. "Is this what you want", I asked her? Your children are in heaven with JoJo and mama Bri. Face it! You knew all about that day. Why won't you believe now?

Bri shook her head no and started backing away from me. Angela smiled, grabbed Bri by the arm and ran out of the building. I tried to run after her and Ricky held me back. "I can't lose her Ricky", I said. Everyone formed a circle, joined hands and began to pray. Great! I thought. A bunch of sinners praying, yeah, like that's going to work.

BJ and I returned home to see if Bri was in her room. There was no sign that she had been to the house at all. Bryan Sr. arrived shortly after we searched the house for Bri. I ran to the door, thinking it was Bri. Not my lucky day it seemed, because it was Bryan asking BJ if he was ready to go.

"Go where", asked BJ?

It is my weekend to have you over, so grab your things because you are coming with me and Bambi, Bryan said.

I want to stay with mom this weekend dad. Aunt Bri is missing and we need to find her. Anyway, I don't want to leave mom alone.

Get your things BJ! It's my weekend. Your mother is a big girl and can handle things on her own. She probably needs some time to herself to think clearly. Genesis, tell him it's my weekend and he has to come with me. Don't make me call the police. It doesn't have to be an issue unless you want it to become one.

I told Bryan to promise me that he would keep BJ out of danger. He replied, like you kept JoJo and laughed sarcastically. Go on BJ. I will be fine and you know where to find me if you need me. I kissed my son and shockingly allowed him to walk out of the door.

Houston Community Center

Alien Alert! Alien Alert! Beware of the aliens. Every citizen must be vaccinated to prevent alien possession of your body and mind control. Your government is using every possible resource to fight against these aliens. Report anyone you encounter that has not been vaccinated. There are alien life forms living amongst us and abducting our children. Our leader, the savior, has all Community Centers administering free vaccines. Get vaccinated immediately for the safety of our community and human preservation. Rejoin the human race. Make a stand against aliens. GET VACCINATED!!!

Form one line. We have enough vaccine for everyone. No pushing! Next person in line, come this way. Do you accept the savior as your god, yes or no? You must answer before we can administer the vaccine. I understand that you are hungry and the good savior will provide food, shelter and work for you and your family. It is a painless procedure, one little stick and all your problems will be over.

"Did you hear that BJ", asked Bryan? Come with me and get in line. I am your father and I know what is best for you. Your mother means well, but she is losing her mind these days. All the fight has gone right out of her. She is even nice to Barbie, I mean Bambi. We already came here and got our vaccinations and we brought you to get yours today. We want you to come and live with us. So man up son, it is just a little needle. Now let's get in line and do our duty to protect our country and way of life.

41

Bryan pulled for the door to open and BJ took off running across the parking lot. He was running for his life. He did not stop running until he reached home. BJ urgently opened the house door. Out of breath he'd gasp while trying to speak. "Mom we have to go now, right now. We are no longer safe here." Dad and Bambi tried to make me receive the mark and I ran. They have already received the mark. He will be coming for me and he is going to end up turning us both in to the authorities. He thinks he is doing the right thing and that you have lost your mind. He means well mom. He just doesn't know what he is doing.

I did not rush. I was in another world, thinking. It seems the more I struggle to get closer to God and no matter how many attempts I try to make to release the anguish, Bryan is always right there. He is always popping up to remind me how much I despise him. She finally spoke and told BJ, "Okay, let me grab my bag. We knew this day was coming. I didn't expect it to come this soon. I thought we had time to find Bri. I know she is going to return to the house when she comes to her senses." Joan didn't raise any fools and she would never leave her children behind, I muttered softly. I knew my mom would not leave any of us behind on purpose and I was finding it quite difficult to leave the only place that Bri might come.

BJ raised his head and said, "God help me please! Mom we have to go, now. Give me your bag and I will put it in the car." BJ took the bags to the car and came back inside for me. He could tell that I was preoccupied with something on my mind.

He asked, "What is it mom? What are you thinking?"

I could not hear him talking. I was deep in thought and even deeper was my contempt for Bryan as it fueled beyond my control. I couldn't believe that this man, my ex was going to cost me finding my sister. Hadn't I been through enough because of him? I wanted to kill him. I wanted to wait there for him to show up and I wanted to kill him. My daughter's father, the saint who so graciously married me, the love of my life, my hero, my husband, the asshole who screwed my best friend in my bed, the jerk who was too tired to drive me and my mother to my grandmother's funeral because he had a date with his lover, the superman who pushed me down when my leg was broken because he had too much to drink, and now the doting father who attempted to defy me and give my son the mark of the beast, I wanted to kill him!

I told BJ to drive to the church and I would be there soon. I told him there was one more place I wanted to look for Bri. He believed me, gave me a kiss and left. I on the other hand, sat there in the dark and waited. I waited for my husband to come home. I walked to the kitchen and got the biggest knife I could find. I was finished with this man. I wanted him out of my life. I regretted the day I met him.

I heard tires pulling into the driveway. I walked and stood behind the entry door. I had already unlocked it in anticipation. There were three knocks on the door and then it proceeded to open slowly. He stepped inside. I could hear a female with him. Good, I thought, I can take Bimbo Barbie out at the same time.

I slammed the door behind them. I wanted them to turn around. I wanted them to see it coming. My anger raged, I drew the knife and proceeded towards his chest. He grabbed my wrist and tried to subdue me. The light came on and I saw it wasn't him. My daddy stood in front of me helping Bri to stand and walk. I dropped the knife and told them that we had to leave. We got into his car and drove to the church. No one asked about the knife and I never spoke of it again.

CHAPTER III

Once we arrived at the church, we took Bri inside and laid her on a cot in front of the first pews. BJ knelt by her side and one of the members had medical experience. They began to care for her wounds as best they could. My father and I went into the entry way of the church to talk. It had been seven years since I had seen his face.

He looked surprisingly well for the type of life he had led. It looked as if he hadn't aged a single day since the last time I saw him.

I stood there, face to face with him. Thank you was the words that finally came from my lips. Thank you for bringing Bri home. I wanted to ask him what happened to the leap year, but I didn't. I was actually happy to see him. I no longer had my mother to advise me and was feeling vulnerable. He was someone I could trust to protect and care for us. He is my dad.

"Where, how did you find her? The question seemed to entrance him. Something was different about him. He appeared nervous and unsettled about something. His eyes lowered as he shook his head slowly, rubbing his index finger across his brow continuously. It was as if he was pondering what he was going to say. He had never been the type of man to give thought to anything he would say no matter who it inflicted pain upon. He was always straight forward and very stern.

He retired as a Master Sergeant from the United States Marine Corps. I guess he went insane after his return from the Gulf War. One war too many it seemed. He had been a Marine since before

I was born. We moved constantly when I was young. Except for the times when he would go overseas. That was when Brianna was born and mom said that she wanted us to have a stable life. I guess you couldn't call him a dead beat dad because he always sent money home.

Once he retired, he never came back home to live. He lived life as a vagabond on the streets, under bridges and at the VA. His visits were always short and sweet, in and out. My mother never said a bad thing about him. She didn't really have to because we formed our own opinions of him. At least I know I did and it wasn't pretty and probably wasn't fair, but I needed him to be there with me. I was always afraid someone would break into the house and kill us all. I tried my best to be the strong one for my mother and not allow my fear to show.

He raised his head and I saw a single tear roll down his left cheek. He looked into my eyes and started speaking. He said, "I was in line at the community center when I saw Brianna enter the building. She didn't recognize me. She passed by talking to a woman. I could hear them arguing about the vaccination. Bri decided not to receive it. The woman seemed very upset. She started yelling and pointing at Bri. She screamed out alien.

She said Bri was an alien. After that the panic started and everything started happening so quickly. I lost sight of Bri for a moment. Everyone wanted to leave the building, but the police reassured everyone that everything was under control.

They would not allow anyone to leave. The very same police officer stunned Bri causing her to fall right in front of me paralyzed. He used a Taser on the back of her neck. I bent down to pick her up and another officer pushed me back against the wall. She was just standing there, bothering no one. She looked startled as the woman called her an alien. She started laughing and before I could do anything, everything went haywire. She didn't even see it coming. Two more policemen came and they picked her up, carried her to a black car and placed her inside the back seat. It wasn't a police car. At least it didn't look like one to me. I found out where they were taking her. I tried to explain that she was not an alien and that she is my daughter, but no one would listen.

I followed the car to some type of facility. It had double barbed wire electrical fencing about ten feet tall all around the perimeter. The building resembled a hospital of some sort. There was an armed manned guard shack at the gate. I asked about visitation and was told there was none at that location. I knew then, she was a prisoner of war and I had to do something fast.

I returned to the community center and inquired about a job at the facility. I used the guards name as a reference that manned the gate. I remembered it from his badge. It took two days to get an interview. During the tour of the building, I saw Bri and where she was being held. She had been scheduled for execution. She had already been tortured and severely beaten. The place was a hellhole and smelt of death.

A man was beheaded as guards cheered. He was beheaded for being an alien. Those people were not aliens. They were Christians and some were Jews. If these people were aliens, they were the most peaceful aliens I ever heard. They never fought back. Even those they set on fire never fought back. The guards kept their clothing, jewelry and other types of trophies to number their kills.

He shook his head again and said, "Anyway, I could not bear the thought that these barbarians were going to kill my baby girl. So I hid myself in a closet until night fell and the guards changed shifts. I stole a uniform and pretended to be a new guard." I located Bri in a 6 x 6 room with several rats nipping at her skin. She was practically out of it. She was naked with whip marks from her head to her toe. Her toe nails and fingernails were missing and bleeding. There was dried blood on her nose and lips and blood on the floor where she sat. It was quite obvious that these were sick bastards. She was raped and sodomized but I couldn't tell how badly.

There were guards standing there peering through the window and laughing each time she tried to fight off one of the rodents. They were wagering on if she would scream out before death. Their conversation was not about killing aliens. Their conversation was about killing Christians and Jews.

One guard said, "One day our world will be rid of all of them." Another one commented that Adolf Hitler died too soon. But that guard was laughed at and mocked. The first guard said, "Our new leader is the true god. He will definitely perfect Hitler's sloppiness. He is the savior, our god and we will destroy the nonbelievers under his rule. They all agreed and gave a salute to the new leader's name. I saluted and said I was told the girl in the cell would be my first kill.

I told them that I could probably get her to tell me where other Christians were hiding. They laughed and said beginners always think they can torture better. She would not say a word and we gave her every opportunity through numerous types of persuasive devices. She is strong willed that one. I broke her as much as possible without killing her. She is scheduled to be beheaded tomorrow.

She will probably be happy death finally comes for her. I might test out that shocking wire on her once more. It was pretty funny to see her nipples get hard. I know the pain was turning her on; it definitely had me hot and bothered. They began to laugh as they walked away. A guard turned back towards me and said, "She is all yours. Have at her now because tomorrow she dies." Then he tossed me the keys to her cell.

I could barely believe what I was hearing. I felt my knees buckle and hid my face. I could barely breathe. I wanted to die myself for not having ran after her and making her stay with me. All of a sudden I started puking and dry heaving. "How can this be true", I cried. "Why are you letting this happen", I asked God? I would have screamed it out, but my voice was too occupied inside of my head. I shook my head no. This is all wrong I thought and began sobbing louder. My strength was gone. We were all going to die. My father stood me up and as I hugged him limply around his neck, he continued to tell me the horror Bri had endured. "You need to be strong Genesis", he said and continued speaking.

I got her out of there as fast as I could by hiding her in the trunk of my car as I passed the guard shack. All I could think of was your mother and how I had let all of you down. I drove over the first hill, pulled the car over and placed her in the back seat of the car. She told me your address, just before she passed out. She has been through a lot and I don't know if she will make it. I am so sorry Gen.

BJ walked over to me to tell me that a prayer session for Bri was starting. I looked at my son and told him that I wanted him to meet his grandfather. I gently turned BJ around in front of me and said, "Dad meet your grandson, Bryan Jr. BJ looked over his shoulder at me, searching my face for a sign of what emotion I felt for this man.

He appeared as a baby looking for his mother's hand before crossing the street. He wanted to know if he should exhibit joy, concern or dislike for this grandfather he had never met before and who was left behind. I mustarded a faint smile which was the clue he sought and it assured him that his grandfather was a safe person to acknowledge. My smile brought a smile to his face as well. "Delighted to meet you sir", said BJ as he extended a welcoming hand for the taking.

His grandfather did not shake the hand of his grandson. Instead, he grabbed BJ and pulled him towards him for a bear hug. He wept holding on to his grandson and then apologized for getting all choked up. I found this to be a strangely odd emotion coming from a man who had just told the most horrifying story I had ever heard concerning the torture of his daughter and only shed one tear. I couldn't understand it and did not have the mental capacity to try to figure it out.

Ricky distracted me with news concerning Bri's condition. Everyone surrounded Bri in prayer. They prayed to Almighty God for his healing hands to cure Bri. They prayed for guidance and understanding and for protection. They needed a miracle from God for Bri to live. She was in desperate need of a doctor and a hospital. Although she had always been a fighter, her desire for living was fading. Several people were living at the church these days waiting for a miraculous intervention. I wasn't so sure about that any more. I needed something and I needed it right then.

Ricky told me that he heard some people talking about safe houses. He was concerned about getting Bri the necessary help she needed. "She should be the first to go", he said and I agreed. Tell me more about these safe houses. They are Farmers Helping Christians, FHC. It is just a group of good people who received the mark to survive, but are on the side of God's People. We need to set up a map and mark each farm house that is participating. Maybe they can have a signal for each family to look for that identifies them as a member of the FHC. This didn't sound logical, but I was game. What else were we to do and besides, my head was feeling fuzzy.

"When should we start out for the houses", I asked? It isn't a solution to our problems, but it is a welcomed bandage. Who did you get this information from and can they be trusted? Ricky nodded yes and I went into action. I started with list of names of those who needed the most care. We spread the news to the church members and the excitement grew rapidly. A good hot meal, clean clothing, medical attention and a bed to sleep on sound like a dream come true. Especially for those who had been out of their home since the rapture occurred. Eventually, everyone will have to make a stand for or against Christ Jesus.

The eclipse is tonight and the world is already undergoing a major change in ideology and values. The United States of America, USA is on the verge of becoming a socialistic government and the individualist by no means could endeavor upon self-expression. Personal battles between the individualist and the government *were lost before they could begin by the inability to exist without the basic needs for survival being met. The government is controlling every resource and has eyes everywhere.*

We all gathered at church and sat in prayer. Complete chaos started all at once. Planes fell from the sky, cars crashed into one another and the world went black. We didn't die. We didn't know what to expect to see in the light of morning. We knew that each day would be new. We were adding to history and a new beginning. Two weeks passed and we continued our routine.

We as a nation did not fully recover from the blackout of the eclipse. A new clock, calendar and order formed, making a scared world of unsaved residents, slaves to materialism. It also caused people to behave as government robots, gullible enough to fall into the arms of the first leader that offered a false sense of security and normalcy. The only battle to be fought was one within self, mental and spiritual. Unfortunately, the majority of the world was losing the battle to materialism and the anti-Christ.

Residents of the USA would either conform as one under the communistic control of The European Union or perish at their hands. Russia and China had already pledged war against the USA and they held a major power within the EU. The EU consisted of several states and was growing rapidly with one currency and mostly everyone of one mind. The Roman Catholic Church governed by the Pope was controlling all religions. There was only one following accepted, the following of the Pope whom had declared himself as God's only chosen Prophet of the New World Order. He called to all Christians to follow him.

The thought of making it to Heaven had become sanctuary for the left behind Christian believer. Through faith in the word of God we knew Heaven was our new home according to Revelation. We understood the fate of our journey and whether it was physical or spiritual the end of evil was sure to come. We, as new Christians, had all come short of the rapture and had no desire to be found short on the Day of Judgment. The light had been taken away from the world and we waited anxiously upon his return.

My father watched everything as I watched him. I just could not shake the feeling that he was hiding something. I wondered if mom felt this way before he left us. There was something about the way he over reacted to hearing the news of BJ and showed little to no remorse about Bri that concerned me greatly. He told me that I had to be strong. What is he good for if I have to be strong?

He stood in the back of the church whenever BJ was teaching the word of God and watched everyone. Did he think we were all aliens, and if he did, why did he bring Bri back? Did he mean what he said about getting information from Bri? Was this his way of proving himself to the beast? I began doubting that he returned as a doting father figure for me and Bri. Mom would know, but she is not here and I don't trust that easily anymore. So, I watched his every move.

Bam, bam, bam . . . There were several knocks on the door. Immediately, I thought we had been compromised. We'd spend each night at different church locations attempting to make it hard to impossible for the police to catch us. Bam, bam, bam . . . The knocks came again. A tremble took over my body and my mind was anticipating sweet death.

Open up in the name of our leader!!!

We had been compromise, I thought. I went towards the door and my father said, "I've got this?" I stood behind the door to listen to what he had to say.

He opened the door and a man started questioning him. I recognized the voice. It was Bryan. He asked if his son was there, Bryan Jr. Some people call him BJ, he said. My father told him yes, BJ is here. I couldn't believe my ears. Bryan stepped inside and said, "I need my son now. He is a minor and I have filed for custody. My blood boiled behind the door. I could not help myself. I spoke out. Bimbo

Barbie had not quite entered the building and at the sight of me, she retreated towards their car.

I closed the door and told Bryan that he had no right to take our son away from me. BJ is old enough to make his own decision on where he wants to live. Bryan replied that I had brainwashed BJ and that I continue to taunt him with illusions grandeur. I had been accused of a lot of things, but taunting my son had never been one of my traits.

Bryan, I pray to God to forgive you for the things you have put me through. All of the shame and pain of being lied to and cheated on by you was unbearable, but I did it. I was laughed at by family and friends while trying to protect your dignity and honor. I lost so many of my relations behind me playing a fool and staying with you as long as I did. I tried for the kids to make our marriage work, and I became tired of being the only one putting any effort towards reconciliation.

You disrespected me in my own home after our divorce several times and allowed your bimbos to do the same. And if all of that isn't enough, you take our son to get the mark of the beast, which would be his one-way ticket to hell! What is wrong with you? I use to think it was me who needed help, but now I realize that it is definitely you. For someone so smart, how can you possibly behave so much like an ignorant jackass? Why won't you admit when you are wrong and ask for forgiveness instead of trying to over talk me and belittle me?

I thank you for what you did for me, but God knows I wish you had not married me. We did not love one another. We put each other through hell. You never wanted to marry a Black woman. Although you are bi-racial, you always had your eyes and your heart set on White women. Everything from the past is okay now because it happened and there is nothing we can do to change it. The fact remains that we did get married and you didn't even try to make it work for the kids.

BJ is not your son. You know he is not and so do I. I will fight you in court and bring out the truth if I am pushed. Blood and DNA don't lie. What was I saying? My anger was getting the best of me. Why can't this be a nightmare? Someone please pinch me quick before I never wake up.

BJ came into the room and ran to Bryan, giving him a big hearty hug. "I knew you'd come around dad", he said with excitement. I just knew it! Bryan looked at him and replied, "What do you mean by come around son?" I am here to protect you and take you away from these evil people. They are corrupting your mind son. We have a god now. Our leader is here on earth with us. He can do all kinds of things and he only wants to take care of us. You have read in your bible about him coming and he is here. These people are trying to deceive you. They want you to wait for some UFO, probably their mother ship. Bryan laughed at his own joke, but he was the only one laughing.

BJ took a few steps back and said, "The antichrist is NOT Almighty God! He is the deceiver! Dad don't you see him for who he really is? Stay here with us and learn the truth".

I quickly turned and looked at BJ. Did I hear him correctly? Did he ask his dad to stay with our group, my group? No! I screamed beyond my control. No! Besides I said after regaining self-control, Bambi is waiting on you. All three men looked at me at once, my father, Bryan and BJ. "You called her by her name", said Bryan. Maybe we will stay for a little while. I will go and get Bambi.

BJ was teaching a lesson that had to be inspired by God. He spoke about the Garden of Eden and about the tree of life and the tree of good and evil. Unlike when our pastor spoke, I heard every word he said. He said that Jesus is the tree of life and Satan the tree of good and evil. Satan, once the most beautiful of Gods angels, became jealous of Jesus because he was to receive a key flock favored by God. The second creation of man was to be Gods chosen people. So Satan stole what was meant for Jesus by beguiling Eve. Man was

53

given the freedom of choice and the choice made in the garden was the wrong choice.

Like a bad movie, we watched it happen again and again in the Bible. God was trying to get everyone to see the truth. Cain and Abel, Jacob and Esau, and Isaac and Ishmael were three of the known brothers in biblical history that contemned their brother or their brother's position and inheritance. No man knows the mind of God, so no one knew Gods Plan. God came to earth in Jesus to regain his flock and set straight the hand of time.

He has told his children that he is a jealous God and there will be no other God before him. He told them that if they destroy his temple, he would rebuild it in three days. They crucified him to destroy his temple, the body of Christ, and he arose from the dead in three days. God has said his sheep will know their shepherds voice. Jesus went to hell to regain the key flock. Today he has sheep throughout the world and he is calling them home. Can you hear him? Stand up if you cannot hear the voice of your shepherd. Beware of the wolves dressed in sheep's clothing among you. Know them by their works and their words, for a man cannot serve two masters. Satan's followers will try to destroy the body of Christ, which is his flock, but Jesus has already paid for his sheep with his blood. Like Cain and Ishmael, Satan has been cast out. God made this world and it shall have one ruler and one flock. We shall overcome. Like my Aunt Bri, we shall overcome.

Bryan looked around the room. He murmured numbers as if he was counting. I will wait for BJ to finish, I thought, and then question Bryan on why he stayed. When I turned to find Bryan, he was gone. He and my father were gone.

Everyone began to stand up and gather around BJ to thank him for another great sermon. I went looking for Bryan and my father. I found them standing just outside the backdoor located behind the church. I could hear them talking.

CONTEMNED

"So, what at are you doing here", asked Bryan? My father replied that BJ is his grandson. Bryan was startled. You're Genesis dad? He laughed and said, "You're the loser!" Then he laughed again.

"Why are you here", my dad asked Bryan?

Bryan said, "I am here to get my son before these idiots get him caught and killed. I already lost my daughter behind this foolishness and I refuse to lose my son too. If you are his grandfather then you know what it means for him to become a productive man in this world. He will die if we don't intervene right now." He is being brainwashed by Genesis and those religious fanatics. Anyways, how did you get her to accept you knowing you have the mark?

I almost compromised my position. I thought my heart would stop beating for a moment. I felt myself quietly gasping for air. I remembered my father always wore gloves that exposed only his fingers because of weight lifting when I was a child. I never even wondered why he wore them now. Oh my God! What do I do?

Genesis doesn't know I have the mark. No one knows except for you. "What are your intentions on getting the boy out without being noticed?" He is their leader. He kind of reminds me of myself, the way he takes charge and his dedication. Bryan became arrogant and rude.

What dedication do you have? You abandoned your family. BJ is nothing like you! You sold out for food you reject! Let's see just what your daughter and grandson thinks of you after finding out that you have been perpetrating a fraud. Maybe you are their traitor for status with our new leader? Either way, you are going to be exposed. Get out of my way old man!

I heard scuffling. I looked around the door to see my father kneeling over Bryan's body with a bloody knife. He held Bryan's head up and said, "You won't be saying anything to anyone." He was still alive, but his throat and neck was sliced and blood was squirting from a vein on the left side. I back away slowly, trying not to make a sound. I was frightened and yet trying not to be frighten at the same time. I wasn't saddened by Bryan's death, but I was disturbed by it. What am I doing? God help me I whispered to myself. I need to change my life. I need to change the way I feel about my past. I feel so lost. I should feel something about Bryan's death and yet I only feel relief. God please help me figure out where I am emotionally, mentally and spiritually. How did I get this far into sin? Why I am not saddened I haven't a clue?

"Oh God, here comes Bimbo Barbie, I mean Bimbo, I mean Bambi, no Barbie, I don't know what I mean." I felt sick and light headed. From this point on I want a new beginning. Deal with me God and give me a fresh start. I want to be a decent mother and person. I want to be like Jesus to be deserving of your love and grace. I realize this is not about just me. It is about everyone still here, lost and trying to find their way to you. Please God forgive me for my sinful heart and mind. Grant us all a new beginning with you. So many emotions were running through my mind. I turned to see my father entering the room with BJ and I collapsed.

I awoke alongside of Bri. BJ was fanning me. "Mom, are you okay?" I heard him asking continuously as I came back to consciousness. I sat up and asked, "Where is your grandfather?" BJ said, "He is helping Bambi look for dad." I thought I was going to faint again. Now that you are awake, I will go help them find him. I want to know what he thought about the sermon.

I quickly told him No and to stay with Bri. "I will go and find him, I mean them", I said. I started rising up from the cot when my dad came walking back into the room. He announced that Bryan and Bambi had left. BJ's head sank down in disappointment and he said, "I wish dad would have at least tried to understand. Maybe he will come back."

I thought that his dad needed to learn when to keep his mouth shut. But that wasn't something he had to worry about any more. I didn't believe Bambi had to worry about anything anymore either.

I wondered if he had sliced her throat too and nausea over took me.

What did my dad want? Why was he here? I was afraid to ask the questions and afraid of finding out the answers. A part of me was grateful to this murderer and another part was terrified of this man I knew as my dad. I was the only one who had seen what he had done. Do I tell everyone and cast him out? Why should I be there for him, just because he has done a few nice things lately and maybe because he's my dad? The fact remained that he is a murderer. He was no better than the policemen who had Bri locked up and scheduled for death. Time was moving much too fast for me to think too long about any one thing. My mind needed to rest for a little while. I had been awake for days, finding it very difficult to sleep. I fell asleep that night out of pure exhaustion. I had fought a good fight, but my eyelids lost the battle.

I picked up my Bible and turned to Matthew. I must have walked Jesus all the way to the cross, reading in the New Testament. I needed answers and I knew the only way to figure out what to do was to read his words and try to follow his footsteps. I fell asleep with the Bible was across my chest. I saw the face of Jesus and his eyes were blood red, piercing straight through me. While I slept, I dreamt I saw a scarlet robe fall to the floor from out of the sky and Jesus face disappeared. I was immediately taken into the sky, spun around and tossed back into the cot. When I awoke, my body was soaking wet from head to toe. What was happening to me? Did God mean for me to turn around and change my ways? I don't want to be tossed down from heaven. I just can't be rejected twice by God. So, I started in Genesis, reading my Bible every day. I had to change my ways, my mind set, but first I had to find out what was blocking me from his sight.

I had finally set up the first members to journey for safety. Bri was feeling a little bit better. She was eating and talking with the others, but any movement she made was still a struggle. All of her strength had not been restored yet, but she was determined to do her part. She agreed to leave with the first group only because I told her I needed her to oversee and report back to me any changes that we might need to make in future journeys. I wanted her away from dad and for her to watch over BJ.

The first group consisted of all the young teens and mothers with their newborn babies. Our group now consisted of many members from other churches in the area that had fell short on faith. I never thought that mothers-to-be would be left behind. I heard the road was narrow. I guess I had no idea how narrow God meant by narrow. We must be either hot or cold, no lukewarm temperatures allowed and I had been very lukewarm. My guess was that everyone here had been a lukewarm Christian.

I found a quiet place to sit down in my confusion and lick my wounds so to speak. I felt so alone in my attempt to be strong, never wanting my mother more than at that very moment. Just then, two familiar voices came from behind me and brought a sincere smile to my face.

"Look at her sitting there as if she is the only one going through something," said Tonya. Sandra laughed and added, "Yeah, like she has lost her best friends." I couldn't help but laugh as I stood to give them both a hug. Girl do you see all the sinners in this place? Tonya looked at Sandra and said, "We are all sinners, you nitwit!" See, you made me sin right then. I can't get to heaven being around you.

Sandra said, "If I was going to be left here, I should have given my number to LiquidPoetry." Is he here?

"I haven't seen him", said Tonya and I can pretty much tell you the location of every male in this place. "EboniSkye is here. I saw her at the altar earlier."

"What?" I couldn't believe it. "I thought she had it all together. I thought she knew the answer." I wasn't aware I said that out loud.

"The answer to what question", asked Tonya?

"Just the answer to stuff", I said. "She just seemed wise to me."

We were together again. I didn't know if this was a good or bad thing. I loved these two very much, but none of us made it to heaven. We are all falling short somewhere. I wanted to tell them about my suspicions concerning my dad, but I decided not to mention it. Instead, I suggested for us to go and introduce ourselves to EboniSkye. If she is as real as she seems, she is going to need some real sisters to talk to.

That's for sure Tonya said, because there are some really fake people out there in the group. "Let's go and say hello ladies."

EboniSkye was standing in a corner watching Bri and writing something on a piece of paper at the same time. She watched as Bri gathered her bag and organized others things for their trip very slowly when she thought no one was paying attention and how she would speed up, taking a deep breath to endure the pain as she pretended to be in ship shape when others were around. I didn't know why she was watching Bri at the time until I heard what she had written.

"Hello" was the first word I said, as I approached her. My name is Genesis and these two characters are Tonya and Sandra. We use to go to DJ's Blue Note Café to watch you and Liquid Poetry perform. You are awesome. Why are you here? I mean, I'm sorry. It is really none of my business. I don't know why I won't stop talking. "Someone help me, please."

Tonya interrupted and said, "She is your biggest fan." We all started laughing. EboniSkye spoke and said to call her Eboni. Finally, I was meeting the person who could answer my questions.

Sandra immediately inquired about Liquid Poetry and Eboni told her that he and his family were taken in the rapture. "What a waste", replied Sandra, followed by a just kidding.

59

So what were you doing when we first approached you? Were you drawing my sister, Bri? It seemed like you were staring at her. Eboni turned the paper around and there were words written all the way down the sheet. "What does it say", I asked and Eboni began to read.

THE WHISPERER

The brown leaf appears at the window before the storm
Diligently tattered and worn
Like the Son of Man until she is dead
This leaf has no place to lay her head
Unable to contain God's precious tears
Separated too early by the shears
The cuts, scrapes and holes she now possess
Were once whole in love and happiness
Planted on good soil her roots went deep
And into the leaf nourishment did seep
But branchless leaves blow to peculiar places
Reaching strange and unfamiliar territories on regular bases
Considered lost and consumed in sin
Always flying within the wind
The slightest breeze starts its motion in flight
Walked upon by the darkness, crushed in the night
Either gathered with others or left to die
This leaf still flies
In constant repeat are seasons in this world
Once again we see the life of a girl
A story told of numerous lives lost
A cry unheard since the Holocaust
Jesus is her strength as she protects love unseen
No longer present, yet reigning supreme
The love for her children, mother and niece
The love which desires Jesus return and peace
She speaks to him within her every sigh
And by her side He is nigh
In her eyes lay a soul obsessed
Longing for his word to say she is blessed

Worldly things do not make her to stumble
Is this intelligence or madness she mumbles?
Either gathered with others are left alone
She would have flown
Until the day her home returned in sight
Reached by day throughout a long night
Precious this leaf does appear
To those who hold leaves so dear
Either gathered with others or left to die
This leaf will fly
She shall answer the call when it occurs
God commands the wind, He is the whisperer.

~EboniSkye~

Wow! That was good. People had gathered around while she was reading. Bri looked as if she understood every word had been written about her feelings. She felt like her emotions had been exposed although Eboni never discussed her inspiration for the poem. Eboni could see Bri's nakedness and immediately clothed her by redirecting all of the crowd's attention on to herself and walking away, knowing they would follow her every step. She looked behind her to see Bri exhale in relief and then she smiled as she turned back to face the crowd. She was exactly what I had expected, a wonderful person. So why was she here with us?

Tonya said, "She is nicer than I imagined. I bet you anything she is here because of a man."

Sandra started laughing and said, "You are probably right! That is the reason we are all wondering around here looking stupid."

I told her that she might be looking stupid, but I look intelligent. Tonya agreed and we all looked at each other and laughed. My laughter was cut short when I saw BJ coming.

BJ had become close to his grandfather. He came walking into the room with his teenage disciples by his side. I couldn't help but

61

wonder if any of these boys had something to do with the raping of the girl. There were a large number of teenagers and young adults left behind. Probably because most teenagers had never heard of the word rapture before it happened. They were so confused by the world about what really mattered from what did not. Most of them were searching for the type of love and understanding that only the love of God could provide them. Yet, they wanted to be accepted by their peers. And let's be honest. The cool kids or rather the in crowd were the ones with money and little to no scruples and on the reverse side, the rebels without a cause were cool. There are the rich kids acting grown-up in order to gain acceptance and love, and the poor kids fighting to create a world in which they will have self-worth and love. Few teachers and fewer Christians are around to lead and guide by example. Leading by example has been the only way for years after taking discipline and religion out of the schools. Once they find the truth of God's love, they are more faithful than adults.

The thought quickly left my mind when my dad walked in looking for Bri. She was falling for his charming demeanor. The fact that he rescued her had blinded his past abandonment of the family in her eyes. I guess it had blinded me too at first, but only for an instant. How could mom forgive him so easily? She had to work constantly when he left. And Bri, I know his not being around had a lot to do with her different phases of life. She was gay one day and straight the next, every other day in high school. She was looking for love anywhere and everywhere because of his absence from our lives. I said I never would marry a man like him and ended up marrying someone worse. I don't have to worry about him anymore.

Sandra noticed my dad when he entered the room. Damn he is good looking! Bri hit the jackpot. Tonya hit her with the back of her hand on the arm and said, that is her father you dipstick. I couldn't help but giggle a little. Sandra was in the hormone line for seconds when God was passing out brains. I heard my dad ask Bri if she was packed and ready to leave. He said that he would escort the first group to the safe house. My mouth dropped open. This cannot happen, I thought. How would I know they arrived safely? He is a *murderer who has the sign of the beast hidden under his glove. I could not stand by and watch him take them away.*

Bri said no. You stay with Gen dad. She will need you here especially when Bryan returns. He smiled and said okay. He said take care of yourself and my grandson. Bri replied "I will" and he left the room.

Tonya could tell I had become distracted. What's wrong with you she asked? We stared into each other's eyes for what seemed to be an eternity when in actual time it was merely seconds. For a moment our souls connected. I wanted to cry and tell her everything as if she was my mother, but I kept my composure, smiled and said, "Nothing girl". She knew I was lying, but the first rule of being 'girls' is being strong. We ridiculed weak women, always crying over spilled milk. They'd better wipe it up and keep moving, "Woman up", we'd say.

Our lives had not been a bowl of cherries although as adults, we make it look like it is a bowl of cherries with Cool Whip on top. We learned this attitude from our mothers. They taught us that in order to achieve, we had to be ten times better than the next person. Dress like a millionaire and demonstrate class and dignity and let's not forget, marry well. I remember my mother telling me that men all have the same parts, so if I find one that is decent and works hard for me, that is my keeper. She said marry him for the papers, but realize he only sees your relationship and himself as a leased Rolls Royce with no true possibility of ownership. Most men think of themselves as the answer to what every woman wants and needs. She said one man per woman is enough and to buckle up for the ride. There are slow and consistent rides and there are fast and exciting rides and then there are dangerous rides. Slow and consistent may be boring, but it is up to you to liven up your relationship. Don't liven him up too fast, because when you do, the comfortable ride will change around the corner and he'll become a rollercoaster in the dark and you won't be the only rider.

God if I had just listened to all of her wisdom that I mistook for craziness, I would be in a much better place today. I would have been in the rapture. Instead, I am in a bad head spin, clueless of my next move. I thought I was living. I thought I was grown way too early. I had to do things my way. With every step I took, the more confused I became. Listening to people who knew as much if not less than I did and allowing them to give me directional advice. W.T.F!!! I should have been more careful!

What am I thinking? Obviously sticking with my girls wasn't the ticket before the rapture, so I need to make a move for myself. I am going with Bri and BJ. I need to get away from here. There has already been a murder and God only knows what else is happening with all of these people. I am going to pack my things. I am leaving tonight.

CHAPTER IV

The truth is and shall always be what we choose to believe. Sometimes it is and sometimes it isn't the truth!

Everyone is dressed in dark clothing carrying a backpack containing water, clothes and necessities. My dad entered the room to say bye and to give BJ a talk of encouragement and a hug. I hid my pack behind some boxes. The remaining people were to go to a new location tonight. I talked with Ricky and mentioned my concerns about some of the congregation. I told him I was leaving with my family. He understood and expressed his own desire to leave the group as well. He said people had been talking about leaving the group and receiving the mark. Remember the lady who had the baby? She took her baby and left one night. There are several sneaking away in the night lately. Sooner than later, they will turn the rest of us into the police.

I was so wrapped up in my own troubles, till I hadn't noticed the crowd thinning. I asked him how many had left and were there any among us with the mark? He stared as if looking straight through me and shook his head no slow and nervously. My dad walked up behind me and said he needed to talk to me for a moment. Ricky quickly excused himself and hurried off in the opposite direction. I could tell he was hiding something. He knew something about my dad. I didn't know who to trust anymore. Ricky was like a girlfriend of mine. We could always talk about anything.

My dad took my hand and said he was glad to be standing with me through this hard time. I smiled and told him thanks. I didn't know what to say. A part of me wanted to believe him to be sincere while another part of me was yelling run for the hills. I couldn't tell good advice from bad advice and I didn't trust anyone. The one thing I knew for sure was to not let him know I was leaving.

I found Sandra and Tonya and gave them a hug. I wished them luck on their journey. Tonya said," we will see each other soon" and Sandra laughed and said "yeah, as soon as we get to the other church".

Tonya smiled at me and said, "I thought God took care of babes and fools, why is she still here?" I had to bite my lip to keep from laughing. We parted for the night when Ricky came for me to help him put out the candles and check the rooms for anyone left behind.

The lights were out and everyone was on their way. I grabbed my pack and flashlight and set out. It wasn't until we reached our first rest stop that I spoke to Bri and BJ.

What are you doing here, asked BJ? Bri simply smiled and said I am glad to see you Sis. BJ resented the fact that I left his grandfather behind. I took a deep breath, shook my head, took my son by the hand and walked away from the crowd. I told him that his grandfather had the mark and what he had done to his dad and Bambi. He pulled away from me and said he wanted to be alone for a while. I forced a hug on him and left him sitting there to collect his emotions. He knew he didn't have long before I would be back asking him to get with our new group. He knew I expected him to man up. I taught both of my children what the phrase man up and woman up meant. I told them I expected them to man and woman up whenever they felt they were too grown to take my advice. I was trying to scare the hell out of them so they wouldn't make the same mistakes I made.

I sat down and told Bri everything I knew and about my suspicions. She cried a little and said that she wished things were different.

She wanted him there. She said we could save him and change his mind.

Bri, he has received the mark of the antichrist. He is lost forever now. I believed he was behind the people leaving the church. Either he was telling them how much nicer life would be for them, or he was killing them. I didn't know which one to be exact. I was just happy he was away from me and my family.

I knew we had to move. We needed to reach a safe house as soon as possible. I didn't have to call out for BJ because he came to me. I asked him if he was alright and he said yes. He didn't say I will be, he said yes. Thank God this boy learned something from me.

BJ said, Mom I need to tell you something important. He told me that his grandfather knew the location of the first safe house, but that he did not think he knew the locations of the others. We needed a new plan. Somehow we had to bypass the first safe house without being noticed. The plans were to sleep in the woods until morning because of the nightly patrols and national curfew. We were supposed to arrive at the first house at the busiest time of day. I gathered everyone together and announced that we would be moving all night. Hopefully tomorrow we will be long past the first not so safe house. I wish I could tell them they had been compromised, but maybe all of them weren't trust worthy. I didn't know who to trust other than BJ and Bri.

Kurt Seland wrote **The Post Rapture Survival Guide** *and I provided a copy for everyone in our group. The importance of his words was needed by all of us. I had not realized how difficult life after the rapture would be until now. I was lucky enough to find a copy and used the last of the ink in the church printer to make more copies. I tried not to be afraid after reading aloud to everyone, but between the tears and stuttering over certain words I think it was pretty obvious that I was afraid. There is no safe place in the world. There is no peace. I longed for my mother's wisdom and strength. I longed for her faith.*

This is what she was trying so hard to protect me from, but I thought I had time. I thought that playing internet games was more important than reading my Bible. I did not make time for God and now, He is my only thought every micro second of each day. We are being hunted like animals. I want to go and see the two witnesses. They know the way to salvation and they can speak directly to God on our behalf. We need to listen to them and pray with them. We need to get to Israel. I had read in my bible that they would be there. I wasn't sure of when they would arrive in Israel. I only knew that they would be there. Some say it will be Moses and Elijah preaching at the wall. Men of strength and of God and the strength I needed to continue living.

Once everyone gathered together, I noticed a few familiar faces. Tonya, EboniSkye and Ricky walked up together. After the meeting, Ricky said, "There was no way I was staying there with your father. There is something very strange about him and all three of us sensed it. I think he is one of them Gen." I looked at them. I wanted to tell them I felt the same way, but how could I tell them now. I left them there with him.

"What are you doing here?" asked Tonya. You felt it too, didn't you? And you weren't going to say a thing. Some friend you turned out to be.

"Oh yeah, and just where is Sandra, Ms. I'm such a loyal friend", I asked? Eboni stood in between us and told us both to cut it out. She said this is a serious matter. We are all going to do what we feel is best for ourselves. This isn't a time to sit around and sing Kumbaya and hang with your friends. This is the time to be serious minded and release negative forces that are blocking you from your goal. We are all trying to get to heaven here. Do either of you think fighting is the way to do that? I don't remember who apologized first or why the tears wouldn't stop rolling down my face. All I knew was it was time for us to start back on our journey.

We needed to hide. Every day we would cross more and more dead bodies. The criminal element was at an all-time high. We were so hungry and trying desperately not to commit a sin against God for food and water. Scripture was our bread and God provided for our thirst. We were not so prideful any more. We had learned how to wait on the Lord. We knew that death was ever so presently knocking at our door. Our only prayer was please don't allow us to die without you Heavenly Father.

We walked through wooded areas as much as possible until we reached Buffalo Bayou. It is the main waterway flowing through Houston, in Harris County. It begins on the west side of the county near Katy and flows approximately fifty three miles east to the Houston Ship Channel and then into Galveston Bay and the Gulf of Mexico. This is it I thought! The bayou is our ticket out of here. Ideas started rushing through my mind, followed by several questions. "How do we get away from Houston, Texas, the United States without being caught?" I posed the question to all three of them standing there.

"Not by airplane", said Tonya?

"What about train", asked Ricky?

"By boat", said Eboni. We should go by ship!

"You're right", I said. All we have to do is follow the bayou to the ship channel or Galveston Bay. We informed everyone that it was time to move out. We knew better than to announced any of the plans to anyone again.

Along the way, the bayou passed through rich private communities. We found all types of inflatable boats, floating tubes and other devices along the path in their yards. They wouldn't miss any of it. They probably don't even remember they have any of these things. Normally I wouldn't be caught dead on the bayou and these crazy rich people actually float on it. That's just nasty.

It was Bri who came up and said, "I have an idea, the cruise ships. If we could get aboard a cruise ship from Galveston to Mexico, we would be well off the route. Those cruises leave out all the time. I once saw the crew members debarking. They left the ship from a side door." We must collect money from everyone and any jewelry that can be used as bribery. Amazingly enough there was not a single complaint. I guess history prepared us well for this moment. The worst part was realizing that each day we spent escaping by faith, was rendering us closer and closer into an area of no return. Families were being separated due to their need and dependency of materialism. There was no video dating, designer clothes, jewelry, computers, cell phones, toiletries or make-up out here. There were no tents, guns, knives or bow and arrows.

The bayou water was horrible, but there were no complaints as we traveled for miles throughout the night. By morning we reached Galveston Bay. The most difficult part of our journey was from Texas City to the Bay. I didn't think we'd all make it through the breezeway of Ship Channel Bridge, but we did.

The wind and the currents were horrible. It took hours to travel one mile through that water without being seen. I cannot say if our quest had turned into unwarranted paranoia, but I can say that pure determination was pulling us through. We were focused on one common goal and we used all of our efforts and strengths to stay on task. One step at a time we were heading for our destiny. God was making a way for us. We had not been forgotten. We weren't ready when Jesus came like as a thief in the night. We were too busy pleasing ourselves then. Now, we were preparing ourselves for the war and our chance to prove our new found understanding and faith in him. We had a lot to learn about how to be true Christians and live the faith. Our mission was simple, find the ship that would get us away from the USA and closer to Israel.

We used every cent we had to get aboard a ship. Some of us posed as kitchen workers, housekeeping and passengers. Our head count was twenty-seven. I remembered back at the church when we first met the other church members, our total number was sixty five members. Slowly they left the group. Some were caught and others went willingly. The only reassuring thought was that we had heard of other groups trying to find safe havens.

I still had not heard a word about my dad. I heard about a man fitting his description helping other people get to safety. I want to believe that it is him. I want to think he has had a change of heart and is really trying to turn his life around. I think I will keep that thought and one day I will share it with Bri and BJ, but not until we reach safety.

We gathered and said a quiet prayer that we would all make it to our destination alive and well. We didn't know where the ship was going. We only knew it was leaving in three hours. There was a lot of work to be done. Name badges were made, uniforms were issued and guest passes with rooms were assigned. God had led us to the right individuals and although we paid with all of our material worth, we could feel safer and rest our bodies for a while.

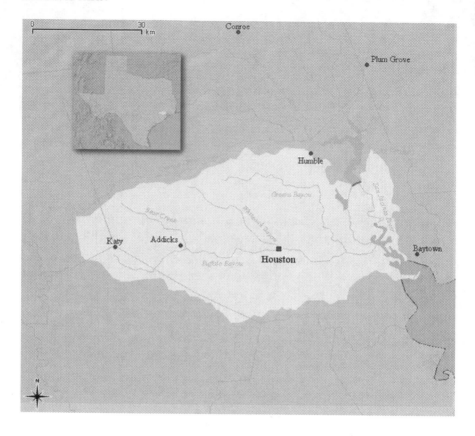

Buffalo Bayou Path to Galveston Bay

It didn't take long to find out the ships destination. My faith was reinstated. We were heading for Europe. That night I went on deck and stared out at the moonlight glistening across the ocean. The wind blew a warm breeze so I let my hair down from its constricting ponytail for the first time in what seemed like months. I felt guilty for enjoying this moment of ecstasy. I guess it was around three in the morning when I heard a voice ask me if I was enjoying the view. I turned to see the figure of a man. He stood around six foot two, muscular build on an average size body with salt and pepper hair. He had broad shoulders and the most soothing Italian accent in his voice I had ever heard.

Yes, I said. The view is magnificent. He was dressed in all white like an angel sent from heaven. I couldn't help but think of Sandra for a brief moment. She would have been all over him by now. I smiled at the thought and whimpered for leaving her behind.

"What a beautiful smile you possess", he said as he came along side of me and leaned on the railing. I glanced at this middle aged Greek god and shook my head. Anyone who looks that good could not possibly be good for me. So I said goodnight and started to leave.

"What is your name", he asked? I am the ship's captain and would love for you to sit at my table for dinner tomorrow night. The ship's captain was the only words I held on to after he asked my name. My palms began to sweat. I was afraid we would be discovered. Why had I come on the deck? I tried to think of something to say that would make him find me repulsive. I hated to do it. But, this situation was calling for an emergency reaction. The captain, of all the people I could have bumped into in the middle of the night, I bump into in the captain.

I tossed my hair around smoothly as I turned slightly to face him. "Did you say captain", I asked? I remembered how being too aggressive turned men off faster than a cold shower. Without giving him a chance to respond, I quickly commented, "A captain should know his guest." I smiled at him and said, "I am honored to meet you sir. I walked towards him in a flirtatious manner and extended my hand. When our hands touched I felt warmth in the midst of my belly and I forgot for a moment about trying to turn him off. It took me a moment to regroup.

"I, I, I am not much for big crowds which is why I came out at this time tonight", I was stumbling over my words like a tongue tied teenager. I was thinking that he had to be pretty busy being the ship's captain and all, so I asked him out at and inconvenient time of day. "Why don't we find a secluded little spot tomorrow onshore in the Caribbean to get to know each other better?" I was positive he was hit on constantly by women of all ages. The average man is always afraid of an aggressive woman. "This should send him running", I thought.

He smiled and said he would be honored. "I know just the spot", he said. "It is a spa, my treat." "You look a little tense", he said as he reached up with his hands, slowly turned me around and began massaging the back of my neck and shoulders. "May I", he asked as he briefly paused? I was thinking no, but yes is what I heard come out of my mouth. Oh it felt so good! I didn't want him to stop. I had forgotten about everything and everyone for a moment. My flesh perspired to his touch. He actually captured my air in some way. "There", he said. You will enjoy the spa. It is a place where a lady can be treated the way she should. I hadn't had a single drink, but I began feeling intoxicated. Was it his cologne or the sea air? The odor was sweet and mild. It calmed me with the sound of the waves and his voice. He released me softly and said, "I will meet you at 7:00AM, right here." I repeated our time to meet and went to my room.

We only had two balcony rooms for everyone. There were at least seven people in the room. A room accommodated comfortably, three people at any given time. I laid down alongside of Bri, Tonya and BJ. The four of us shared the bed.

Bri asked. "Where have you been?" When I told her what happened she giggled lightly and said if only he would have come along a few weeks ago, huh?

Tonya rolled over and sleepily said, "She is still going for the captain." I shushed them both and said goodnight.

CHAPTER V

I awoke at 5:00 AM from a nightmare. Normally, I have the most beautiful dreams, but not this time. It started with me talking with an old friend while we were shopping at some department store. We were both laughing about what our husbands were going to say about the price of the outfits we had found. Evidently it was a good day shopping because I returned home with several bags from several stores. My dream skipped all the other shopping, to me coming home, and then to me seeing my husband who was happy that I found so many things that I liked. All of a sudden we were at another house, the country house in St. Martinsville, Louisiana. There were distant family members there and night time was starting to fall. It looked as if we were moving our things out. Some man was angry about it and said they will never leave alive. Something told me to go my car. Once in my car, I heard people with dogs coming and I saw the doors lock on their own. The car started driving away. I scream and asked what about my husband, but the car kept on leaving and that is when I woke up. That dream scared me scared me because of the angry people chasing after me. I haven't been to the country house in years. It sits on 28 acres and far off from the road, but I still would not go there. Wish I knew what it meant.

Seven in the morning came early, and although I arrived before seven, he was waiting for me against the same rail as the night before. Wow!!! He looked like a dream in the moonlight, but he was a dream come true in the sun. Tonya had followed me to deck and quickly brushed past me to ask him a question. I wanted to laugh, but I simply smiled as she gave thumbs up behind his back.

"What a magnificent morning", he said. My sun arose when you arrived on deck. These are for you. From around his back came two red roses, one with thorns and one without thorns. The rose without thorns is me, Nikko, to show you I mean you no harm. The other rose with thorns is you, and today I shall remove the thorns from your life. I may not get them all today but if you will permit me, I will spend my life removing them all. "Is that alright", he asked?

I wanted to rip his shirt off, straddle him and make him the happiest man alive. My body and mind had already sinned. My lips wanted to taste his so badly till I could barely concentrate. "Good morning", I said in my after sex voice. Lead the way Captain, my captain.

He smiled and said to just call him Nikko. It is short for Nicholas Stephano Arrigiano III. Oh no I thought, "His name even sounds hot." Maybe I should cancel, make an excuse and just leave. My will power is just not strong enough for a test of this magnitude. I swallowed hard and gave him my hand and once again I was in paradise.

He talked all the way to the bungalow. He was my personal tour guide telling me about the history of the island. The taxi stopped in a small village by the seashore. We walked on the sand around a bend and there it was.

It was beautiful. There shimmering in my sight was a secret waterfall, amongst huge boulders hidden behind a small bungalow between sister hills. Down the shoreline of white sand were old fishermen sitting on lonely rocks in hopes of catching their evening feast. Caribbean music played in a far off distance as the warm wind continued to blow. Inside of the cabin was a fruit basket with cheese, crackers and a bottle of white wine. There was a masseuse and two women. One woman led me to a room to change into a towel and the extravagant care began. Nikko watched as I was pampered. He would smile at me as he ate from the basket and sipped his glass of wine.

The massage was last and it put me to sleep. I awoke alone in the cabin. On the bed was Nikko's shirt. I put it on and walked outside to find him. He wasn't there, so I strolled down the shore thinking, "What does this man want from me?" Why is he being so nice? As I looked back towards the cabin, I saw him standing barefoot in the sand. He wore only his white baggy pants which were rolled up over his ankles. There he stood waving and smiling. He beckoned for me and I did everything I could to control myself and not gallop towards him like a thoroughbred. I figured this was a debt that I didn't mind paying. I mean, it is only right to pay your debts, right?

Genesis In The Caribbean

"How do you feel", he asked?

"Wonderful", I replied.

We sat on the porch looking out at the ocean.

"Please tell me your name", he said. Embarrassed that I hadn't already done so, I said, "Genesis, my name is Genesis and my friend's call me Gen."

"It's very nice to meet you Gen", he said with a smile. We sat and talked about everything pertaining to each other's earlier lives. We laughed, cried and sat silently together for hours. "It is almost time for us to prepare for our return to the ship", he said as he rose and helped me to stand. I stood awkwardly and fell into his arms, his muscular comforting arms. I felt lost. He took my hand and led me inside. I was trying to follow his direction. While he was out he bought me a sundress and dinner for two was on the table with candles burning. I changed from his shirt and put on the sundress.

"How did you know it would fit me", I asked him. He said that the ladies picked it out when he took them back to town. When we sat for dinner, he pushed my chair in, placed my napkin and took his seat. Lobster and veggies with fruit for dessert was dinner. We talked more at the table after he said grace. He married his first love and she and his son and daughter were taken in the rapture. He expressed his loneliness and his gratitude for my company.

We arrived at the ship after dinner and we stood in the same spot we had met. He thanked me for a wonderful evening and kissed the back of my hand. I clinched his hand, pulled myself into him and kissed him goodnight. He smiled and stood silent. It was like tasting sparkling champagne. I stood silent looking into his eyes before I asked if he would be available for breakfast or lunch tomorrow. I wanted him to say breakfast. I wanted to spend the night in his arms and wake up beside him for breakfast. I don't want to sound too forward, but I needed him tonight. I took a long breath and waited for his response.

"I would love to have breakfast with you Gen", he said. He held out his hand and I submitted to being led to his room. When the door closed he stared into my eyes. "I only want to hold you tonight. You are safe with me", he said as he caressed the side of my face with

the palm of his hand. Nikko held me close and tightly all night long and it was the best sleep I ever had in my life.

He ordered room service the next morning and we ate in bed. He knelt beside the bed and asked if there was anything that would prevent me and BJ from remaining in his life as his family. I was thinking yes, but I heard myself say no.

"I want to marry you Genesis", he said. "Will you be my wife?" I was thinking yes and I heard myself say yes. I did not want to leave his presence. I was in love for the first time in my life. I was in true love. He was everything I had ever dreamt about having in my life. A walking dream come true. Tears formed in my eyes and ran down my cheeks. He kissed them away and said to go and talk with BJ. He wanted to meet him and ask his permission to marry me.

I had always been the person in charge and I always had to think for everyone. I walked to my room without a single care in the world. Waiting for me inside of the room was Bri and Tonya. Well, well. Talk to us. Tell us what happened? You are glowing. I sat on the bed and told them everything.

Tonya said, "I am in love."

Bri said, "If you don't marry him, I will!"

"I will too", said Tonya. "How many wives does he want", she asked?

We started laughing. Have you told him about us and how we are on his boat illegally? What we are doing? I looked at them and said no. How do I tell him and what does one thing have to do with the other?

"Genesis, now is not the time to get selfish on us", they both said in harmony. We are following you and everything you do has everything to with us!

I found BJ in the game room. I need to talk to you I told him. He asked what now? The last time you said that, I found out about my grandfather and dad. I told him what happened. I told him everything and about the way I felt. BJ looked at me seriously and then he smiled and said I will talk with him, man to man.

"Is he a Christian", asked BJ?

"He has no mark", I replied.

This is kind of fast mom. "Are you sure he is who you want?"

"He is who I need", I replied. I pray you can understand.

I went to shower and change in my room when Ricky rushed in upset. What is this nonsense I am hearing about you and some guy? Are you out of your mind? What happens in a weak moment, will you give us all up? What the hell is wrong with you? He didn't give me a chance to answer the first question before hammering me with the next one.

"What is your problem", I finally yelled back! "Why are you so upset? Did you have your eyes on him", I asked sarcastically?

"What", he asked? "I am not gay."

That took me by shock. I had always thought he was a homosexual. Sorry, I didn't know.

"What", he asked again? "What do you mean you didn't know?" He walked up to me and said, "I thought we had something. I thought you knew I liked you?"

I didn't know what to say. This can't be true. I never saw this coming. I struggled with words to tell him that I and he would be a big mistake. Besides the fact I didn't share his feelings, he was nothing of what I needed in my life. I didn't realize anything was missing from my life until Nikko. I had somewhat settled for total self-destruction. He should have known better than to come anywhere near my life. I was a train wreck, thought of as the biggest bitch anyone could meet. I hadn't gotten into a serious relationship since my divorce. In and out were my relations. I didn't want to really know them and they didn't need to know me. My little secrets are what I called them and Ricky knew everyone because I talked to him about each guy. There weren't that many, but I never stayed with any of them. We both laughed about how I'd say goodbye before I'd say hello and walk away as if I didn't care. They had been lonely night companions and that was all. If I had seen him leaning, I wouldn't have allowed him to fall, if only. Either way there wasn't anything I could say to him now concerning his feelings. I wanted to get ready to see Nikko. A few people entered the room. Ricky and I looked at each other and I told him that I had to take a shower. "We can talk later", I said and I closed the bathroom door.

BJ and I went to meet Nikko at the Captains Table for dinner. The two of them had lunch earlier and BJ had rendered his blessing. I had no idea until Nikko stood and made the announcement of our engagement at the table. He knelt before me with a ring and properly proposed marriage and once again I was lost in his soul which was manifested through his bright eyes. Our ceremony would be tomorrow at noon on the Promenade Deck. We weren't to see each other for the rest of the night, but there was so much I needed to say to him before the wedding. His crew members shuffled him off for a bachelor party and Bri, Tonya, Eboni and a bunch of other females rushed me off for a girl's night bachelorette party to replace the customary bridal shower. I figured tomorrow we would talk.

THE BACHELORETTE PARTY

It was the most fun any of us had in a long time. It celebrated life, love and release and a time to lay down responsibilities for a moment and rejoice in having made it this far. We celebrated all throughout the ship with every female onboard. Around eleven o'clock the women from our group returned to the room to continue our private party. We sat in a circle and shared stories of our lives . I tried not to miss Sandra, but I did. I missed every female that left the group. Together is strength and separated is insecurity. We cannot think for one another, but we can understand and clarify each other's thoughts.

It was story time. We were set with wine and room service. A few of the stories were similar. The perfect marriage and kids and yet they still missed the rapture. One woman said it was her greed that made her miss the rapture. I had to have everything money could buy. I ran with the Jones. I had plastic surgery every year after forty to tighten, lift or expand something. I exercised so much I started feeling like my sons hamster. I was on my treadmill longer than he ran on his wheel. We laughed with her, not at her, because we had all done the hamster wheel scenario.

She went on to say that she didn't realize at the time how much she was trying to hold on to youth. The real problem was my fear of death. I figured by staying young looking and on the go, I could cheat death. I was killing myself trying to stay fit and young for a husband who still threw me away for a younger model. So, I went out and got me a younger model too. Why I do not know. I started looking like his mother in very little time from all the stress he put me through. Everyone called me a cougar. Honestly, I couldn't even look my friends in their eyes from the embarrassment. I had no one to blame but myself, but I blamed everyone else besides me.

I looked in the mirror one day and looked at him waiting for me in bed and decided that was enough. I was beating my body up on the outside, while he was beating it up on the inside. I wanted to look beautiful on the outside and lost the inner beauty I never cherished that which was the beauty of godliness, purity, honesty and love. It was an even exchange, godliness for bad and sometimes evil behavior. Purity was exchanged for raw sexual passion and intercourse, and honesty lost out totally, my whole look was a lie. That lie was so big till I didn't know who I was anymore. Finally, love I exchanged for hate. At first it didn't seem like it, until I met a woman who was true to herself and everyone around her, including me. She gave love so freely and innocently till I started hating everything about her. She was beautiful inside and out and she was everything I was not. I never really hated her, my evil ways just made me think I did. She wasn't afraid to love me and she is definitely the reason I am here today fighting to save my soul.

"Wow", said Bri. She took a deep breath and said, "My turn". I got pregnant in high school and aborted the baby without telling anyone except the doctor who did the procedure. She looked at me and said you were in college. It was easy to get away with since it was the doctor who got me pregnant. You remember Carol's dad from around the corner? Anyway, I was Carol's babysitter and her dad was a handsome older man, and a doctor. I thought he loved me. Now I know better. God only knows how many girls he got pregnant. I didn't like myself much after that. I felt guilty. I wanted to have a baby to make everything alright. I knew I was cute. Every boy in school wanted me and my sister, but Genesis wouldn't give them the time of day. I on the other hand did. Once I found the one I wanted to have kids with me, we were like rabbits. We got married and moved to his family's hometown. He was only attending school in Houston because his parents didn't know what to do with him in Illinois. I thought it was cool for a white boy to be acting all gangsta. We had two kids, a boy and a girl. Both were born with blond hair and blue eyes. So his family loved them. They did not love me very much. I was called out of my name more than once, accused of trapping him into marriage and had to deal with them constantly trying to hook him up with white girls from his past. They swore they weren't racist and would never use the 'n' word, but the 'b' word they used every time there was an argument. By saying the 'b' word, I mean they called me a bitch. There was no love lost between his mother and me, I couldn't stand her and she couldn't stand me.

Well, the fighting started and became worse over time. He would hit me and I would hit him and so on. He had a job working at his family's business and I lost my job working as a receptionist at a friend of his aunts company. I felt divorce coming on so I moved back to Houston with my kids and filed for divorce. I found a job right away and I had always drunk a bit, but my curiosity grew to other drugs that were available in the underground market. I started smoking a little weed and from time to time I would do a little cocaine. I walked into doors I had to fight my way out of. I was sleeping with men and women. I couldn't make out the difference anymore and it wasn't about love more than it was about sex. I had a need to escape and another to feel good. Drugs and sex fulfilled those needs. But it was a lie. I couldn't see how much I had lied to myself until everything good was taken out of my life. My sister and I were constantly arguing about one thing or another, but my mother was praying for me constantly. JoJo, my niece was even praying for me.

My children were my world and I thought I was taking care of them. I punished his family by taking the kids away and then they were taken away from me. I didn't want to believe they were gone. I didn't want to believe that I was left here and had to be responsible for my actions. I thought that my mother's prayers would get me into heaven. I listened to one of my ex-girlfriends and was about to get the mark of the beast. I didn't want to face the truth yet and was following the lie of convenience. While I stood in that line, I heard my mother's voice. I knew I had to leave there and that if I ever wanted to see my kids again, I would have to wait for judgment day. But once again I found myself inside of a door that I could not get out of. If God had not intervened in my life at that very moment, I would have never seen this day. I have asked God for forgiveness of my sins and accepted Jesus as my Lord and Savior. I am so sorry for what I have put him through.

Tonya said, "You should be sorry. Acting all girls gone wild and not wanting to listen to us when we were telling you to stop. But you did stop and that is all that matters. I could see your faults clearly and yet I couldn't see my own." Gen we always thought that Sandra was following us when in fact, we were following her. She was subtle in her suggestions and would laugh them off. We would call her silly and move on. Sandra came to me the night I left and said we should go and find ourselves a good man to take care of us. I told her that I did not want to look for a man anymore and that I have other things on my mind like how to get to heaven. Besides I said most of these guys are married. She told me that she had been talking with your dad and that he was going to take her out to a real club. She said that he had the mark and that he was doing just fine. She tried to convenience me to go with her and your dad that night. I looked for you and Ricky to tell you both about him having the mark. I found Ricky and we both spotted you tailing the group while we tailed you.

So don't feel sorry for Sandra because she is living her life the way she decided to live it. "Eboni, you saw her leaving with him didn't you?"

Eboni shook her head yes.

I am responsible for myself. I am trying to figure out what I did so wrong to miss the rapture. My trifling husband and my kids went. Girl you know that man couldn't hold a job any more than you can hold volcanic lava. He was always home with the kids while I held down two jobs. I worked six days a week and went to church on Sunday. He expected me to come home and make Sunday dinner. We argued all the time. In my mind I have reviewed those arguments and now I see that I was the one doing the arguing. It just seemed at the time that he said things to set me off. When actually, it was me going off because I felt I should have married better. He wasn't living up to my expectations of a man, but obviously, he was living up to Gods.

I am sitting here listening to everyone so far and the thing we have in common is men who have wronged us and self-contempt. Ladies I thought I had forgiven the men in my life that caused me anxiety and stress, but looking back at the circumstances, I know that I never truly forgave anyone in my heart. God judges the heart. He can see what is in our hearts. You know, I can forgive everyone else, but the men in my life I held accountable in every way. We missed the rapture because of scorn. How does that saying go?

"Heaven has no rage like love to hatred turned, nor hell a fury like a woman scorned."

We all started out with love in our hearts for these men. Time and situations changed our outlooks on life and love. If they were only honest, didn't cheat, worked to provide for all of our wants and needs, knew how to hold a conversation, never blamed us for anything, realized that flirting is part of our nature, weren't violent, kept up the yard, car and the outside house appearance, then life would be fine. We expected men to be perfect as our husbands and they weren't, so we despised them for what they lacked. They were the cause of all of our problems. That was the biggest lie we could have ever come up with. They are about as perfect as we are and we are not perfect. I know where to start now. I have found the wound. Now I need to figure out how to heal it.

"The hardest part is admitting you have a problem", said Eboni. I know you have heard that saying before. It is the twelve step program. I have sat in on a few meetings after visiting with a friend once. I realized they talked about a lot more than drug addiction. They talked about what made the addictions start. You see, God expects perfection from us, but the world which is Satan's playground has made possible every excuse and way out of being perfect possible. It's the same as telling our kids if the lesson is too hard then don't do it. We weren't leading by example.

I became a spoken word artist after traveling the world. I started out young and met a lot of different people with very different lifestyles. I started writing about the experiences. I tried just about everything mentioned here today. I didn't leave a stone unturned, nor a door not entered. I was young with no children and not by choice, so I was bitter. Everyone was getting married and having children that I knew. My life would forever be separate from my friends who became mothers. I watched friendships die over time from early on. By the time I was grown, all of my friends were pirates. Life had taught me that nothing stays the same and that regular people would never be friends of mine. I was a dreaming wonderer. I tried not to get involved with anyone for two reasons.

One was not to hurt them and two was to keep them from hurting me. I just knew how to hide the pain better. They all left and I am sure it was my fault. I was only a visitor in the relationships. My heart stopped bleeding by the age of twenty-five.

I got married later in life to my best friend and was as guilty as anyone else of what Tonya said. I got married when I was tired of trying to climb out of walls I had built to high. We adopted two kids and I thought I tried to make it work. I know he tried to make our relationship work. He couldn't tear down my walls no matter how hard he tried. Little did he know that although I said I would try with him, I wasn't truly trying at all! My heart was just not willing to take a chance on a new person. It was hurt one too many times. I guess once a pirate always a pirate.

So I sit here today without a past and looking forward to each day of the future. I want to go to heaven, but I can't breakdown my own walls. God will show me the way, I have faith and I have done the work. He will send someone with the right tool to release a frightened heart. I was mad at him for a while. It took work, a lot of work, but I got over myself. Now I wait on him. I guess I have to learn to trust people and maybe that is why I am here. How can I trust him if I can't trust him in his servants? You know?

I did know. I knew exactly what she was saying. My heart was burnt by every man I had ever met. Having a son helped me to see good in men again and yet even that pictured blurred. Nikko was different. There was something about him. Ladies I said, you must all think I am totally insane for getting married. I agree with everything each of you have said and I have learned from each situation. Before yesterday, I would have sat here with a very similar story. I forgave my ex-husband recently for everything he put me through, knowingly and unknowingly. I also asked God for his forgiveness. Nikko was sent to me like an angel from heaven. I was trapped too Eboni. I didn't see a way out until he took me by the hand a lead me out of my own maze. He is who I asked God for and he is here. I had to grow to learn that I needed my own personal relationship with God before allowing anyone inside of my life. I accepted God as the Man of my life and He sent me a man for my life.

Every woman in the room sighed. I would never do anything to hurt any of you. Everything is going to be just fine. I need him to lead us. We don't know a thing about Europe or how to get to Israel and he does. I haven't asked him yet, but I will. I want to share everything with him. Neither of us is perfect because we are both still here, but together we will do our best to achieve godly perfection. BJ needs him, I need him, and we all need him. I can finally breathe without pain. I am accepting my gift without question. Besides, he told me everything already. Everyone laughed.

We all laid down for the night. The guys never came in so I guess they slept in the other room. The main guy I was worried about was BJ, but I believe Nikko would make sure he was fine. I rose early to go and speak with Nikko, but so did everyone who was going to stop the bride and groom from seeing each other until the wedding. A beautiful dress was delivered to our room and the ladies helped me put it on. The sundress was a trial run for my dress size because it was a perfect fit. Before I knew it, it was time for the ceremony.

The wedding march played and I walked down the aisle on the promenade deck. He was waiting with the Assistant Captain as the minister. BJ was his best man. I wanted to run down the aisle and I smiled through the whole wedding. When he placed the ring on my finger, he whispered in my ear. I am a Christian too and will take you and BJ to Israel myself. We kissed and it was over. I grabbed his hand and ran him down the aisle and up the stairs to our honeymoon suite. This time when the door closed, there was nothing that needed to be said and we stayed in that room for three days straight without interruption.

We talked on the balcony wrapped in each other's arms. I told him there were twenty-seven in the group and about how we came to be on his ship. He assured me that everything would be fine. He also provided more rooms for the group. Thank God we were married, otherwise my body would have sinned again as I watched this man take control. Where had he been all of my life? I had seen other women with men like him before, not often, but when you see them, you remember them. I watched his every movement; the way his lips moved when spoke, his walk and everything else concerning him. I wanted to familiarize myself with what he needed before he would need it. I was caught in his eyes and peacefully drowning in his soul.

We went to dinner on the fourth night. Tonya looked at Bri and proclaimed loudly, "See, I told you he would survive."

I was red from embarrassment, but could not help but to smile. Nikko laughed and responded to Tonya in the same loudness, "Just barely." Now I was glowing red, but Nikko placed his arm around me tightly and I bury my face into his shirt. "I told you we should not have come out of the room", I said. He just laughed and said, "We had to come out sometime and it would still be the same." Then he whispered to me, "So, it's been awhile huh?" I told him, "Si signore and I am trying to make up for lost time. Can you keep up signore?"

He laughed and said, "I have you covered on that Signora Arrigiano."

BJ came to the table with a silly grin on his face. "Mom", he said, "I have never seen you look so happy."

Nikko pulled BJ towards him for a hug. He asked him if he had held down the ship in his absence. "Yes signore", BJ said laughing and mocking me.

I love you too Bryan, "Now go sit yourself down for dinner you little comic."

Everyone laughed and just before we all sat for dinner, Nikko whispered to me once more, "You complete my life and give it reason. Ti amo Genesis. Voglio passare il resto della mia vita con te. Siete la mia aria."

I didn't know the translation of what he said and at the time it didn't matter. It sounded better than dinner looked and I hadn't eaten real food in four days. Later, I realized he told me he loved me and wanted to spend the rest of his life with me and that I was his air. Words I will remember always.

CHAPTER VI

Days had past and we finally arrived in Europe. We stopped in Portugal, Malaga and Barcelona, Spain. The sites were beautiful. We grabbed a newspaper from Malaga and watched the news as a group. Americans were being asked to return home to the US. Nikko continued to read the paper and concern began to show on his face.

"We need a new plan", he said. We must separate in as many groups as possible and the smaller the group, the better. We will form groups when we reach Barcelona, but for now enjoy Malaga and the security of the ship. Make this a night to remember.

Malaga Spain

The trip took fifteen days total and we still had a long way to go to get to Israel. It is funny how I can remember the strangest things at times. I recalled being in the mall with my daughter for one of the latest fads at that time that she just had to own. I met a guy from Israel who was trying to return home by selling Dead Sea Salt as a job. It was strange the way we met. Inside of a crowded mall, out of hundreds of people, he walked at least twenty feet from his stand, passing several people and came to me. He said he had been waiting for me. He drew a map of a safe place to go to in Israel because I told him that I wanted to be there for the return of Jesus Christ during our conversation. I told him that I could not go to Israel because my life was in the United States, my loved ones, job, house and everything else. Now look at me. I guess it was meant for me to go to Israel.

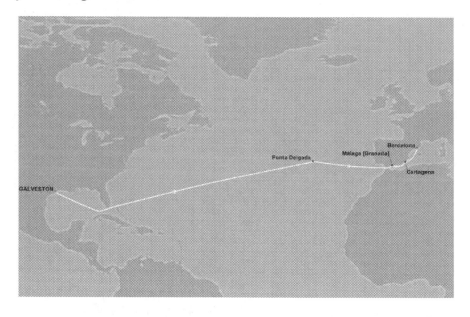

The Cruise Route from Galveston Bay to Europe

We arrived at 6:00AM and debarked. We all went down the beach to gather for a meeting. Nikko told everyone that we would be separating into four groups of seven because it would be less conspicuous than a group of twenty-eight foreign people walking around trying to get to Israel. Everyone agreed that he made sense.

Our group consisted of Nikko, BJ, Ricky, Bri, Tonya, Eboni and me. We had maps from the ship, backpacks and our basic needs to look like tourists. We hugged, kissed and prayed together one last time. We wished each other success on our journeys and agreed to meet in Amman, Israel in two weeks. Our group was heading to Nikko's home in Sicily, Italy. There we could adjust to our new surroundings and figure out what was happening in the world. As soon as we reached the street we could see signs and posters of the new world leader. I thought the US was bad, but not like this. It was like Medieval Times. People gathered around a stage for a public beheading of a Christian. Nikko said his car was parked a block away and for us to hurry while the crowd is gathered. Some of them were drinking beer as if they were at a sporting event. We reached the car, piled inside and drove until we reached France.

The country of France had been infiltrated by Europe United (EU) signs all over the roads and buildings. Everyone in the car was quiet and very nervous. We stopped to go to the rest room and to regurgitate every time the thought of the beheading came back to our minds. Ricky wanted to get something to eat and noticed the method of payment was not with money. The customer's hands were being scanned. We walked away not causing attention to ourselves. Ricky said there has to be Christians here somewhere. We should find them and get something to eat. No said Nikko. We should keep moving. We should be in Sicily in two days. An announcement came over the radio in French. There was a policeman standing on the corner speaking with another man. He said, "It's about time the EU took a stand against the Americans." I was shocked. The French had always been our allies. We looked at each other and decided to get back into the car and leave. Driving at night was very dangerous because not many cars were out during the night. We parked the car at a public place and rested for the night. At first light we were back on the road.

France To Italy

We took a route with no tolls along the coastline. All we had to think about was getting on and off the ferry without being discovered is what we thought. I understood some French from school and all of the summers spent with my grandparents in Louisiana. The New World Leader was making a speech and declaring war against the United States of America. That posed as a problem for all of us except Nikko. I proposed that we adapt to our surroundings. It was time to change clothes, our accents, names and looks. It was time to play dress up, only this dress up was based on life for the winners and death for the losers. I asked Nikko if there was a place we could get passports. He said not to worry; it would be taken care of once we arrived at his home. There was a road block ahead. It was more of a checkpoint of some sort. We were all fine until we saw seven of our friends lined up outside of a car with their hands over their heads. I immediately told BJ to cover his ears and lay his head in his lap. We were at the checkpoint. Ricky and Tonya were kissing in the backseat. Eboni and Bri were engulfed in some make believe language in conversation and BJ couldn't be seen because his head was down. The policeman bent into the window to ask for identification when the first shot was fired. He rose up and turned to look. I could hear them pleading for their life and I heard another saying the Lord's Prayer when another shot was fired. I wanted to scream. Nikko asked the officer what was happening. The officer just waved him on to go because he didn't want to miss the commotion. Nikko slowly drove off. As soon as we were out of the policemen sight, he pulled the car over.

I screamed silently in-between the sobs, tears and puking. How could anyone do such a thing to innocent people? Tonya and I puked in harmony while Bri, Eboni and Ricky said nothing and did not move from the car. Nikko called us back to the car and said we must leave the area as soon as possible. Tonya tried to stand up and fell back down to her knees. This can't be happening she said. This cannot be happening she yelled looking up at the sky! Nikko ran from the car and grabbed her and carried her back to the car as she screamed out why God why? He held her tightly and looked into her eyes and told her that if she does not stop yelling and get inside of the car, we will be next. What was happening seemed unreal. Russia and China had joined forces against the USA. I wanted to return home just to see that no one was attacking my homeland. No one can destroy the United States I thought and mumbled to myself, but the thought made me ill again. I started seeing black spots and the feeling in my legs was leaving. Nikko had gotten Tonya in the car just in time to catch me before I fainted. He placed me in the car, revived me and said we will be fine if we keep our heads. He quickly kissed me and started the car.

Rome Italy

We made it through the ferry without any issues. The ferryman had known Nikko since he was a boy. We were starving when we arrived in Sicily. Nikko was a very wealthy man. His villa was breath taking and he had several servants he employed. We sat to eat, but my stomach was still refusing to hold food and as perfect as Nikko was, I found his fault, money and power and his dependency on it. He was raised wealthy. He was the only heir to deep rooted family money. I watched as he took charge and met all of our needs. When we were alone I asked him why he was left behind. He reminded me of the parable of the rich son. He said at the time he wasn't ready to leave it all behind. Now, I am.

My father worked so hard to keep our family wealthy and I thought it was my job to do the same. I made it possible for my family to be free to live a good life, attend church and give to the poor. My life however, was based on the financial and business end of the relationship. I will not lose my new family. I will be with you every step of the way. When we leave here, I will be leaving it all behind. My money contributed towards the office of the new leader. It disgusts me now to think of it, but it was the only way to keep my family safe and away from the mark of the beast. I lost the rapture behind money Gen, not greed. I know my faults and I do not intend to make the same mistake twice.

And just like that he was perfect again in my sight. We all slept well. I was afraid to leave the comfort of the villa. Tonya asked. "Why can't we stay here?" I feel safe here she said as she started to cry. She wasn't alone. We all cried except for Nikko. He reassured everyone, we would be just fine. Faith he said, have faith. There was so much death and disease everywhere, beautiful places filled with malicious people. I tried not to be afraid, we all tried. Ricky said, "Thank God I kicked that smoking habit. I would probably be at four packs a day right now." Eboni laughed and said I think we could all use a glass of wine.

The servant brought us all wine and Nikko said, leave the bottle and bring another please. We all smiled. I told BJ that even he was allowed to have a glass of wine. He smiled and said, "Let's, get this party started." Everyone laughed for a moment. It felt good to laugh. Bri said for everyone to wait. Let's pray and thank God that we have made it this far. Let's pray for our relatives in the states. Father God, we thank you for your guidance, she said. We all bowed our heads and listened as Bri prayed. After we all said Amen, Bri asked, "Who is better off, the seven of our friends that died or us?" Everyone was quiet again.

We all knew where we were headed, but there were misconceptions of why. I pulled out my bible and read from Revelation. I explained that although everyone is going to attack Israel, it is the only place that will be protected by God Himself. This is why we are trying to get there. Life might not be better, but we might remain alive to see the coming of our Father. There are more people there to help than anywhere else in the world. It will be hard to live there with war and poverty, especially since none of us has ever experienced either. My advice is to focus on the lord with all that you are. He will provide. He did not bring us this far for no reason.

We finished drinking and headed to bed. The first night was very peaceful. It wasn't until the second night that servants woke us up saying the police were looking for the Americans from the ship. They are at the gate the servant said. We woke everyone up and

Nikko had the servants take us to the barn to hide. They covered us with hay in the dark and ran back to the house.

The police searched the house and questioned Nikko. He asked where they got such a ridiculous notion. The police said they questioned one of the crew members they found and before they killed him, he told everything to spare his life. Nikko laughed and told them that they had been lied to and he reminded them of everything he has done for the community. I will be calling your chief in the morning he said. Maybe I should call him now and disturb his sleep as you have mine. The policemen said no one is here besides the servants. The officer in charge told Nikko that calling the chief would not be necessary and he apologized for the inconvenience. Once they were out of the gate, the servants came for us. We knew it was again, time to leave.

Nikko owned a yacht which we loaded with all we needed. We were going to try to sail to Israel or as close to it as possible. We spent the rest of the night posing for pictures for our new identification cards and passports. The morning was full of fog which was a blessing for us. We were able to load the yacht without being detected. Nikko knew the police would return. The chief was money hungry and would want to be paid off, but if he could place Nikko in jail and claim him to be a Christian, then he could confiscate everything in Nikko's possession. Nikko brought what he needed for bribery, deeds, money, jewelry, titles and gold. I looked at Eboni and said, "Now you are a pirate, we all are." Nikko ran back inside of the house for a few jackets when he was stopped by the police again.

A servant came and told us that he would be sailing the yacht. "Where is Nikko", I asked? The servant said, "He was detained by the police." Nikko told the police that he was going for a walk. When asked about the fog he commented that he didn't have very long to be home so he wanted to enjoy each moment. They took him to the police station where the chief of police questioned him. The chief of police was not the person he knew. It was a non-Italian man who spoke English with a Russian accent. Nikko tried to bribe him, but it didn't work. He ordered for Nikko to be tortured until *death for refusal of the mark and for being a confessed Christian. All I know is he is being taken to the police station.*

"We can't leave him", I said.

BJ said, "We must leave now mom." If he can, he will come to join us. My chest was hurting. I couldn't breathe. I could feel him. "No", I screamed! No God, "why?" Please don't let this happen. Please God, I beg you, please. I couldn't see for the tears and I could barely speak from the sobbing. I felt lost all over again. I had finally reached emotional exhaustion. My mind was spent and my body was worn. The only strength I had remaining was just enough to put everything into Gods Hands. I fell to my knees and prayed:

DEAR GOD

Father of my soul
See me Father; I place it all in your hands
See me Father, I am lost and I don't understand
My soul is hurting, shattered beyond repair
My eyes are bleeding from the intake of despair
Mother Earth is weeping for she has become barren
Too much destruction with no sense of caring
See me Father; I plant a seed into the wind
Seeking forgiveness from a life of sin
See me Father, in fetal position
Shredded by wolves and left in a bloody condition
Your sheep are few without the Good Shepherd in sight
Blinded by reality and cannot see the light
Help me Father and work through me to lead
Give me the strength needed to succeed
I boldly stand up for you and confess
Show me the way Sir that I may be blessed
My life is in your hands Father; let your will be done
Save my soul I pray of you so I will see the return of your Son.

Amen!

CHAPTER VII

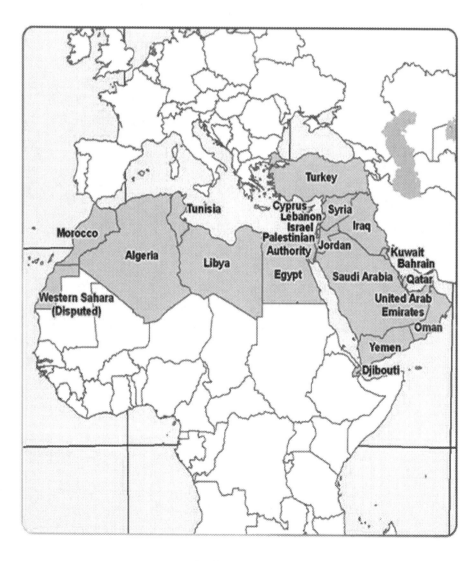

Italy To Israel

We sailed straight to Israel. The fog stayed with us all the way. When we arrived we quickly exited the yacht and changed our clothes to native attire in order to cover our bodies and faces. We desperately tried to hide all signs of our American Cultural Traits. What was I thinking? Why did I bring us here? Israel's condition was a hundred times worse than the United States. People were walking through the streets, military was all over the place. My heart felt like a walking time bomb. Where are the Christians and the Jews who follow Christ Jesus? How are we going to find them? We arrived right before the Sabbath. Sabbath in the states was on Sunday, but here it was Saturday. From Friday at sunset to Saturday at sunset was prayer time it seemed. No one did anything except for pray at the synagogues or stay in their homes.

We kept walking, looking for any sign of Christianity or someone who would lead us to the messengers. A siren went off and people started to scatter. It was a bomb! It blew up a building across the street from where we were taking cover. While hiding alongside of a wall, I saw an American. When he stood up and started walking away, we followed him. Surely he is a Christian I thought. But I thought wrong. He was a Muslim. He met up with other soldier like men and picked up a rifle. We kept walking past him as if we had not been following him at all.

Ricky decided that he and BJ would take the lead. The four of us females followed behind them. We watched everyone. We watched their behavior and mannerisms. We aped their moves. Some of them seemed so happy in spite of all of the chaos. There was a glow inside of their eyes and voices. I heard someone speaking English in the crowd. We went closer to hear his conversation. He was a Rabbi and he was talking to some young Jewish men who had recently returned to Israel from the United States. BJ and Ricky went closer. When the Rabbi was done speaking, the men spoke amongst themselves. One of them mentioned Jesus Christ and was told to be quiet. We followed the one who mentioned Jesus name to a small house. BJ knocked on the door and asked to speak privately with him for a moment. Once he returned to the door, he signaled for us to come inside.

Ricky and BJ explained how we had traveled to get there from the states in order to see the two messengers. The young man's name was Amman and he spoke of his journey. He said the laws in Israel were very different from the laws in the United States of America. He had always been a Christian in America although he was taught his ancestor's ways. He wanted to become a Christian Rabbi. He had followers there in Israel and he was trying to move further away from the city. Why did you come here he asked?

BJ said, "This is God's chosen land and you are his chosen people. God has said he will protect Israel and that it will not be destroyed." The bible says that Jesus will return here to rule. We are here to be near our God. To help his chosen people in any way we can and to learn as much as we can from the messengers. We may not be Jewish, but we have been adopted into his family as Christian believers and we don't wish to be left behind again. For this reason, we came here. We missed the rapture, so whatever was missing in our hearts, hopefully we will find amongst his family.

Amman looked confused at BJ and asked him who had taught him the word? Have you heard of the Illuminati or the secret society, asked Amman? The members are antichrist and have always been a hidden power in the world. They are in the world to confuse man on the word of God. It sounds as if you may have been led here by the deception of the illuminati. The world is going to try to destroy every Christian and Jew who follows the true Christ that remains. The reason we were called home to Israel is biblical; however, it also places a target on our country for annihilation. It doesn't matter where you live. The illuminati will seek out and attempt to destroy anyone who believes in Jesus Christ. Even the most elite are starting to question whether or not the illuminati are of God.

Their deception is monumental. Yes, their ruler was sent by God, casted down to earth to dwell. He was jealous of the relationship God held with man and beguiled man to sin. He caused God to curse the ground which was blessed from the beginning and was found to be good. He initiated the war between good and evil to devour the souls of men. He has many names, but he is best known as Satan the deceiver. He provoked war against God in heaven because of his greed and pride. He has attempted to rob man from their salvation with materialism appealing to their senses of a false need to fulfill their lust of greed and pride. His children are known by the mark of his name to obtain materialism, 666.

The illuminati means enlightened. They know the word of God much more than the average man. So many men seek a tangible leader instead of leading from the word of God. Too many men are still eating from their wives hands instead of leading her in the right direction. Adam and Eve were equals in the garden, but God changed his mind and placed woman beneath man for her sin. The scorn she feels is against God Almighty. She despises His decision; therefore, leaving misplaced anguish and contempt for the men in their lives. She is not angry with man, she is angry with God. Her test of virtue is to abide by the will of God by answering to her husband. Man must overcome their worldly gods and focus spiritually on the Lord God and the blood of the cross of Jesus Christ. The only way to be saved is not to run away, but rather to run to the word of God and believe in His only begotten son, Jesus Christ. Not even the illuminati can touch those covered by the blood of Jesus Christ.

There is so much for you to learn and I will teach you until the messengers arrive. We have three years to wait till that date. The days will continue to regress into the past. Time will be as difficult for us to live now as it was for Jesus to live before his crucifixion. He has sent us a comforter, The Holy Spirit. We can bare all things through our faith in Jesus.

"Wait a minute", said Eboni. I have heard of the secret society a couple of times before today. I never realized they were the illuminati. I know many entertainers they have helped to obtain fame and fortune.

"At what cost", asked Tonya? I read online somewhere at how many stars sacrifice loved ones to obtain public favor. What type *of subliminal messages are they sending out to obtain control over whom the public makes famous?*

"I have no idea", Eboni responded. I received an invitation to join the secret society. The invitation said I showed great potential for success and that others wanted to support my endeavor. I thought it was a joke until I went to a New Year's Eve Party with some friends in New York in 2009. One of them talked about the secret society and how much of a change it had made in her life. She asked me what I sacrificed. I laughed it off because I thought she was drunk and speaking out of her head.

"Who was it", asked BJ?

She is only one of several artist you know and love. Any true artist knows his or her talent is a blessing from God. It is their talent until they become greedy for fame and fortune and then it no longer belongs to them and it does belong to evil. I watched as others rise to success and I thought I had lost my chance for fame and fortune. Later I realized that I hadn't lost my life. I found it. There are so many people who would have sold their soul for a perfect body, money and fame. I was criticized by family and friends for limiting my potential.

"Why didn't you go for it", asked Ricky?

Tonya said, "I would have sold out a few years ago. I was so busy trying to stay young looking and trying to keep my young husband till I know I would have jumped at the opportunity back then."

"I didn't because of my mother", said Eboni. She stood by me through my days of figuring out who I was. I was so full of love and confusion. I love everyone, male and female. It was not about right from wrong. I felt that God loved me regardless of who I loved. It was all about how I loved them. I thought that just because I loved someone, it meant I had to sleep with them. By the time I realized that wasn't true, I could see how many others still believed that. I talked about my dilemma with my mother and she

actually understood what I was saying. She didn't comment from confusion or strife, rather from honesty and love. I can love you Ricky and you Bri, without thinking that I must be in love with you to love you as much as I do. I can kiss and embrace you Genesis and Amman without sexual intent and I can mother you BJ without wanting to kidnap you to make you all mine. The love of God is not a selfish love, but it is deep, long lasting and long suffering. I watched my mother, I learned from her and it is because of her I can now be saved.

BJ asked, "Is it true that they sacrifice their family members for their success?"

Genesis commented, "I heard something about that on the internet. It named people who participated with the illuminati. I never paid attention to it before I saw that video."

"Neither did I", said Ricky. It must have been difficult to give it up.

"Not really", said Eboni. A long time ago my mother turned down a contract for me to model for Calvin Klein. I was devastated. I was one of five models he chose out of hundreds of girls and my mother turned down the five year contract. I thought she was ruining my life. She explained that I would have lost my barely developed soul if she would have allowed me to go with him to Europe for five years. She mentioned that I was not prepared to go out amongst wolves in the world. She said sometimes offers would come that are not of God. They look good for all of the wrong reasons.

I was angry for a while, but I grew to realize that she was correct in her decision. I would have lost my soul. I loved modeling too much. It had become everything to me. It had already become my soul. I lived for it and thrived on the rush of its atmosphere. I loved it. She said that she would not have been a decent mother to sign my soul over to Satan for fame and fortune.

Satan was after me. He watched as I went from modeling to joining the Marine Corps. I did that to spite my mother for not signing the

105

contract. Little did I know that I was going to miss her more than she probably missed me. So, when I was approached as an adult I remembered her words and made the same decision for myself with the illuminati. When she was taken in the rapture I thought I would die. She was my world, my teacher and my connection to Christ Jesus. I was lost until I met you guys.

"Until you met us to be lost with you", said Genesis laughingly? Everyone laughed. Just think for a moment. If we knew then what we know now, we would have been taken in the rapture.

"Yeah, but we weren't", said Bri. What are we going to do now? We have so long to wait for the witnesses. Where will we live? How will we survive?

"We will adapt." Amman said he will teach us. God has been with us this entire trip. We are in the right place at the right time. I am not afraid any more. I am ready to learn all I can and to become perfect in the eyes of God. Jesus said for us to be perfect like him. He forgave us our sins in order to give us a fresh start.

Amman shook his head in agreement. God is Lord and we are his disciples. He holds each of us accountable for what you have been taught and what we have rejected. The things you knew were wrong and sinned without asking for forgiveness and continued to do. So at this moment we will start learning. You will be ready. You are ready.

Perfect! "If that is true then why am I here", asked Ricky? I didn't do anything wrong. If my father had been honest with me about how he felt about my ex-girlfriend, I would not have been caught up in her mess. She made me miss out on going to the Navy, joining the police academy and everything else I wanted to do. My whole life would have been different if it wasn't for her ruining every opportunity I had offered to me. I didn't think God could have taken anything else from me and then he left me behind.

Why do you blame everyone other than yourself? You could have accomplished any goal you wanted to accomplish. You are using everyone as an excuse for what you perceive as your failures. Actually, you are the only one to blame for how you chose to live your life.

I am a teenager and I know that I am responsible for my choices. Just like Adam had a choice and Eve had a choice to not partake in eating from the tree that God told them not to eat of. We all have a choice! We just made bad choices. Don't you dare stand here and blame God for leaving you behind after you broke his commandments. Take on your responsibilities and pick up your cross. Jesus already died for your sins. At least be man enough to admit your sins and ask for his forgiveness from them.

What do you pray for? Who do you pray for? I bet you always pray for things for you and pray for yourself. You are so selfish Ricky! I can't believe I admired you all this time. BJ put his head down and walked to the other side of the room.

Amman touched Ricky on the shoulder as Ricky stood there speechless. Ricky's eyes were going from side to side and he slightly shook his head. He pulled his shoulder away from Amman's hand and shouted.

It can't be my fault! It isn't my fault! She got pregnant and got an abortion three times. I told her we could do whatever she wanted. She made the choices about everything. Can't you see that? Ricky walked quickly from person to person pleading his case. It seemed the more he spoke the more blame he casted on someone else. Now we are here in Israel thanks to you Genesis and we are finding out that we didn't even have to come here.

"Are you seriously blaming Genesis now", said Tonya. Grow up Ricky or at least play with my mind and make me think you can possibly see the truth!

Maybe you didn't need to come, Ricky, but I needed to come. I am seeking God! We are all seeking God and waiting on the return of Christ Jesus, said Genesis.

If God needs me, he'll find me! The same way he found Noah and Moses, said Ricky.

You are not putting yourself in the category as Noah and Moses are you? Noah was a just man. He lived the will of God every day. God was going to destroy it all until Noah came to his attention. He came to Gods attention because he was a just man and Moses was called by God, said Amman. You are blaspheming against the word of God. You should pray and ask for guidance immediately.

If you are so holy, why are you here Amman? You said you are teaching. All I am saying is maybe he has a calling for me too! We were all born for a reason. Mine just hasn't come up yet.

Are you truly being serious or are you trying to be funny? Please tell me you are kidding Ricky. I put you in God's hands. Everything we survived through has been a miracle from God. It's as if you are asleep and have not awakened. There are no more seasons. The time is right now, ride or die and I am riding for Jesus Christ. Amman we thank you for your hospitality. We will work hard for you to show our gratitude for your teaching us. We have the spirit and we need the word.

Amman smiled and said we shall pray for guidance. He told Ricky that he had been so worried about his own happiness that he was not working for God. I was seduced by America's wealth. I was so busy thinking about my pride and the way my neighbors, family and friends saw me that I wasn't thinking about how God saw me. My eyes were everywhere except for on him. My eyes are on the sparrow now! I am not looking at the roughness of the sea because there is nothing I can do to change it, and if I keep my eyes on him it won't affect me anyway.

I was so angry at Bryan. I blamed him for everything going wrong in my life. When you were talking Ricky, a light came on in my mind and my soul said listen! We are the same; all of us in here are the same. Someone else is the reason for our short comings. But no one else really is except for us. These are the issues that we would not let go of, forgive others for, pick up our cross on and give it to Jesus. These are more of the many reasons we are here today being tested through tribulations. We must prove that we can trust in the Lord. We must die to this world in order to live in Gods. It is sad that something so simple made me miss the rapture. Something, I couldn't let go of . . . my anger and shame. It won't make me miss the second coming.

I was just thinking about the words play with my mind, said Eboni. It is so hard in these times to see Jesus. He is a memory from our past. Each day is like a long hard year. No bibles to read, no truth to hear except for the messengers sent to us by God. There are so many lies out there till this trip was worth coming to hear the truth. I wish I had listened to it and read about it when it was easy to do. God I give you my life to receive your words. I wrote a poem for my mother in heaven right after the rapture occurred. It is called Play With My Mind. Ricky I want to say it for you. I know you are hurting. I know how tired you are standing there trying to fight the good fight when all that you loved is gone. Don't lose sight of where they are and whom they are with.

Eboni started speaking with tears streaming down her face.

PLAY WITH MY MIND DEAR LORD

In the quiet moments of life the wind blows love through the windows to my soul
Like the morning dew awaiting the sun this picture of love is too hard to hold
It's only a memory with the fragrance of sweet truth
A life where you and I rejoiced together in my youth
The breath of life I breathe into the void of the air
Are you there?

Are you here with me for this moment in time?
Please God play with my mind.
Someone just called to say you have gone away
If I don't accept it will you stay?
Voicemail, I will leave you a message again.
Ending in my love for you will never end.
I saw a car like yours, I thought it was you
But you probably had other things to do
A breath of life I breathe into the void of the air
Are you there?
Are you here with me for this moment in time?
Please God play with my mind.
My walls are crumbling down as the glass shatters true
Earthquakes are shaking these memories of you
I'm looking up to the sky
Heaven knows these tears I cry
I can't read the signs and your direction's too hard to find
Please God play with my mind.

EboniSkye

Amman said, "God has blessed you with the gift of David." "We shall sleep tonight and tomorrow brings a new day." God willing there will be enough food and water for us all. Amen. I will teach you how to survive each day in accordance to our Father's Will. We will follow the Ten Commandments from the Old Book and learn from its history, our history. And, in the New Book, we will live according to the footsteps of God's Son, Our Savior, Jesus Christ. Pray tonight for the full armor of God to protect you as you learn, for you are the bride maids without enough oil. Together, we shall fill your lanterns and obtain enough oil for our lamps to forever shine for Him. Mentally, we are ready Ricky. Now, we must feed our spirits for strength.

CHAPTER VIII

Three years had passed before we knew it. We were wiser warriors of Christ Jesus. Our lives were being sought constantly but it never stopped us from spreading the truth of Jesus Christ. The number of Christians grew. We were mighty in faith and protected by God. The day finally arrived that we heard word of the witnesses preaching at the wall.

We started out early for Jerusalem. I was excited about seeing Elijah and Moses. I was excited about hearing the words of God and feeling their mighty spirits. I cried all the way there. BJ laughed every time he looked at me. He was hopeful and full of joy.

There they stood preaching. We did not expect the crowd of haters cursing them and calling them the anti-Christ. Ricky grabbed a stone from someone's hand and threw it down.

Don't you know who these men are? They are holy witnesses of God. Listen to them he said sternly, but several people grabbed him and started beating him. They called him an evil representative of the false god. We tried to stop them, but there were too many of them. We were forced to retreat. They killed him and defiled his body. Amman, BJ and some other men moved his body away for burial.

I wasn't sad for Ricky. He had become a soldier in Gods Army. He was not the man he had been three years ago. We feared only God Almighty because we knew his word was truth.

Amman spoke to the prophets and they prayed and talked to BJ as well. My heart felt good. I wasn't worried about my son's soul and I knew we would be reunited with our family soon.

No one cried for Ricky. The deceived laughed and rejoiced because they believed they killed a demon and we Christians rejoiced because we knew he has gone to be with Jesus.

We made camp right outside of the city. This will be our home until either we die or Jesus returns. Each day seems to be getting harder than the previous. The plagues are all around us and there has been no rain since the witnesses arrived. God has remembered us and is with us as he promised he would always be. We have been criticized, spat on and some days tortured for living as Christians. Every chance the followers of the antichrist get to kill one us, they do. They don't realize is that our kingdom is coming and that we are to be kings and queens. We live our lives each day thanking God for each breath as we work to survive and every day we go and listen to the words of the witnesses.

The time period may be approximately one to three and a half days before the end of the Tribulation. The two prophets of God have been witnessing for 1260 days now. Most of the world has rejected God's word. The witnesses finished their preaching and were killed by the antichrist. Their dead bodies shall lie in the street of Jerusalem and will not be put into a grave.

Amman, BJ and some others have gone to try to cover their bodies. They are on display for the entire world to see through the media that the antichrist killed them. This makes even more of the world believe that the antichrist is really God, and that taking the mark and worshiping the image was the right thing to do.

The people of the world are happy that Elijah and Moses are gone because of the numerous plagues against the world and tormented on the people. They had shut off the rain as told in Revelation and it rained not in the days of their prophecy. Now that they were dead, the people of the world gave gifts one to another and rejoiced. They think that now the rain will return and the plagues will cease.

Amman and BJ did not return from Jerusalem. We went looking for them only to the prophet's bodies still lying uncovered in the streets and Amman and BJ in shackles. They were chained and beaten for all to see what will happen to anyone who touched the bodies and defies the antichrist. For another two and a half days, the bodies of the prophets remained in the street and Amman and BJ remained shackled and chained. We tried to give them water and were pushed away by the military guards.

What should we do, asked Tonya? Surely they will die when the world sees the prophets ascend into heaven.

Maybe they will be released out of fear for Almighty God. That could very well happen. We need to be there on the third day. Satan will do everything possible to stop what is about to happen.

It will be incredible to see the two witnesses come back to life. I can't wait to see them stand up on their feet while their enemies actually stand there witnessing the event. Tremendous fear and terror will grip them all. Then they will see that these two prophets really were of God and that the Battle of Armageddon is close at hand.

Then there will be a voice from heaven, which says, "Come up hither." The two prophets of God will ascend up to heaven in a cloud for all to see. So everyone who has been laughing and celebrating because the antichrist (whom they believed to be the true God) has killed the two witnesses, will all of a sudden realizes that the antichrist is really Satan and that they were deceived. All of them that took the mark of the antichrist have committed an unforgivable sin. They cannot be forgiven and will perish to hell. There is no way out.

When everyone realizes the Battle of Armageddon is about to explode and that the return of the true Messiah, Jesus Christ, is about to take place; they will fear for their lives. They will begin to panic. Tremendous terror will come into the hearts of those *that saw the two witnesses come back to life. Some may begin to scream, "No, no, it isn't possible!" But it will be too late. Maybe then we can free Amman and BJ.*

We are almost home. Jesus is coming and the same people, who were giving gifts one to another and shackling Amman and BJ will be so terrified, some of them will fall over dead from fear of what is soon to happen. Just a few more days . . . Amen!

But if I had to do it again . . . I would have listened and been ready for the rapture. Despite, contempt, anger, hatred, lust and everything else that keeps people from walking with Christ and keeping their heads held high, should be released immediately. No one knew the time of the rapture. Be ready or prepare for a nightmare that Jesus can only wake you from!

Matthew 24:34-42 (King James Version) For Verily I say unto you, this generation shall not pass, till all these things are fulfilled. Heaven and earth shall pass away, but my words shall not pass away. But of that day and hour knoweth no man, no, not the angels of heaven, but my Father only. But as the days of Noah were, so shall also the coming of the Son of man be. For as in the days that were before the flood they were eating and drinking, marrying and giving in marriage, until the day that Noah entered into the ark, And knew not until the flood came, and took them all away; so shall also the coming of the Son of man be. Then shall two be in the field; the one shall be taken, and the other left. Two women shall be grinding at the mill; the one shall be taken, and the other left. Watch therefore: for ye know not what hour your Lord doth come.

The trumpet shall sound and I shall report for duty. My name is Genesis and I am a soldier in the army of King Jesus, The Only Begotten Son Of God.

Just a few more days . . .

The Beginning

A MESSAGE FROM THE AUTHOR

The one driving force in my life has been Gods love for me. I desire nothing more than to spread the His word for the remainder of my days. My gift is used to glorify my Lord through poetry, novels, and songs of praise. I wrote this book because of the numerous people who will miss the rapture. I also found it to be self-medicating. My best advice is for each of my readers to follow the Ten Commandments, keep the Sabbath Holy, read your Bible every day and practice the Golden Rule.

I am a Christian Sociologist. All of the resource I have completed has led me back to the simple truth of faith in Christ Jesus. Missing the rapture could happen to any one of us who take our eyes off of the Lord for any moment. The time is at hand, don't be left behind.

For those who did not read my book in time, I have place a copy of Kurt Seland's Post Rapture Survival Guide in the Appendix. May God bless the reader of this book and cover his/ her life with the blood of Jesus. Keep them safe Father and guide them in their travels. May God Be With You . . . Amen!

APPENDIX

THE POST RAPTURE
SURVIVAL GUIDE

by Kurt Seland

THE PURPOSE OF THIS MANUAL IS TWOFOLD

First of all, it is to warn those who receive this manual prior to the rapture of the events that will take place in the last days as foretold in the Bible. Based on what the Bible has to say about future events, nobody in their right mind would want live on earth after the rapture. Hopefully, many will read, believe, seek God, repent and be saved. Salvation is very simple, so simple to attain, in fact, that most people cannot accept its simplicity; thereby reject it completely. However, it is complex because it is life-changing and based on that which we cannot see; it is based on faith. Simple because, Jesus does all the work. If you want to be saved and have eternal life, simply pray in belief and humility to Lord Jesus:

"Lord Jesus, I know that I am a sinner and ask you to forgive me of my sins and prepare for me a new heart. I surrender my life to you."

Secondly, to those left behind after the rapture, this is indeed a survival manual. You still have an opportunity to repent and have eternal life. The same prayer of salvation is applicable to you; the only difference is that you will spend a little time experiencing a taste of hell while you remain on earth.

Let me be really frank with you. If you are reading this manual and the rapture has already occurred, then you probably are not going to physically survive; you most likely will die sometime in the next few years. This manual is about the survival of your soul. You are going to go through terrible suffering. The only question that remains is whether you will go to Heaven or go to hell when you die.

Definition: Rapture—This is the event that will occur when Jesus calls His followers (both gentile and Jewish believers) with a trumpet blast, and in the "twinkling of an eye" they will be removed from the earth and transported to be with Jesus in the heavens.

BIBLICAL FOUNDATION FOR THE RAPTURE

"Take notice, I am telling you a secret. We shall not all die but we shall all be changed, in a moment, in the twinkling of an eye, at the last trumpet call. For the trumpet will sound and the dead will be raised imperishable, and we shall all be changed" (I Corinthians 15:51-52).

"For with a shout, with the voice of the archangel and the trumpet of God, the Lord Himself will descend from Heaven, and those who died in Christ will rise first. Afterward we, the living who remain, will be caught up along with them in the clouds to meet the Lord in the air. And so we shall forever be with the Lord" (I Thessalonians 4:16-17).

" . . . For I am going away to prepare a place for you. And when I have gone and have prepared a place for you, I will come again and take you to Myself so that where I am, you also will be" (John 14:2-3).

EVENTS AND CIRCUMSTANCES PRIOR
TO THE RAPTURE

At the time that this manual was being written, and for the remainder of the time left in this age, the one word that describes the condition of the world is change. All of this change is being accomplished through the work of Satan, as he cannot tolerate anything that originated from God's creation. Originally, the Bible tells us that when God created the world He declared that it was "good." That means that it was perfect and no changes were necessary. Included in His creation were standards to live by that He gave to Adam and Eve. These standards covered everything from how to live in our private lives, to proper domestic relationships, to principles for governing a community. Satan seeks to change everything that God has created and established, thus he has used his power and influence in the world to make subtle deviations to God's original plan. Satan's goal is to establish a world order headed by his protégé (the world dictator known in the Bible as the Beast and antichrist) who will spend his time and effort changing everything to be in opposition to God's will as expressed in the Bible. This is predicted in the Bible in the book of Daniel: "and he will intend to make alterations in times and in law."

POLITICAL

In today's political environment there is no effective leadership in the world. Every nation lacks strong and competent leaders able to deal with the problems at home and abroad. The United States, which has been the world leader for the last 50 years, has steadily lost its influence among other nations because of political leaders in the United States who have no moral center to direct their decision making process. However, this distrust and dislike of government and government leaders is not just an American phenomenon but is a common theme in Europe, South America, Asia and the entire world. Because of this leadership vacuum in the world, there is now an opportunity for a man to arise who is very charismatic, strong, and attractive to peoples of all nations. Based on the prophecies in the Bible such a man will arise, and he will be successful in uniting the various nations to rule as a dictator.

The move to unite the world under one government has been active since the early 1950's, and in recent years this has become more of a reality as many nations have given up their sovereignty to the United Nations during armed intervention of conflicts (eg. Kuwait, Somalia, Bosnia). In these conflicts, the nations of the world contributed manpower and machinery to be used under the flag of the United Nations. The United States of America surrendered its sovereignty in these situations to much weaker nations by allowing its military to be controlled by these nations. In addition to these military actions the nations of the world also agreed to control trade and labor practices with international treaties such as NAFTA and GATT.

There is no dominant nation to provide leadership to the world, thus the stage is set for a man to arise out of the masses to unite the world as dictator.

SOCIAL

The foundational building block of society, that element which has always been responsible for social order and peace, is the family, and it has been virtually destroyed. The family is to be a man, his wife and their children. The man provides for the wife and children, the wife nurtures and educates the children, and the children obey their parents. In a community of families, adults hold the other adults and children accountable for their actions. The family is based on marriage.

Marriage is an institution of God and therefore hated by Satan. The devil has worked very hard, primarily through communications media such as TV, movies, news journalists, and entertainment in general to convince women that marriage is detrimental to their freedom and fulfillment in life. Satan has deceived women into believing that they have the same sexual desire as men and that all differences are the result of culture. Satan has worked hard to divide men and women and have them at war with one another, and because of this, the violence between men and women has dramatically increased.

Civil war has been a constant theme of this age and unrest will continue into the end times: man vs. women, black vs. white, Moslem vs. Jew, Catholic vs. Protestant, Moslem vs. Christian, one Moslem faction vs. another Moslem faction, one black African tribe vs. another black African tribe, nation vs. nation, people vs. people. Whatever divides people into different groups, Satan uses to inspire hate, strife and violence.

Homosexuality and all sorts of perverse behavior are accepted as normal. The world dictator (antichrist) himself will not have the normal sexual attraction to women and may be asexual. Many theologians believe that he will probably be openly homosexual as indicated in the Bible in the book of Daniel 11:37: "and he will show no regard for the gods of his fathers or for the desire of women". And therefore, after the rapture, more than likely marriage will be discouraged or illegal, and homosexual and lesbian relationships highly encouraged.

ECONOMIC

On the economic scene, the trend is toward poverty for the masses with wealth concentrated into the hands of very few people. These controllers of the wealth will be the kings of commerce and banking and also be the power behind politics of the world. Small businesses are merged into larger companies and the larger companies merge with themselves to increase profits. The result is huge multi-national companies that have no allegiance to any community, state, nation or people, whose only allegiance is to increased profits for management and shareholders. The result is workers who are little more than peasants and presidents of companies who are more and more like kings. It will be these "kings" who usher in the world dictator to protect their wealth and power. Expect all commerce, buying and selling, to be controlled by a mark on the right hand or forehead of every person who wants to participate in the economy. Only those people with the mark will be able to buy and sell, but the consequences of taking the mark is eternal damnation (Rev 14:9-11).

Therefore don't take that mark. You will have a very difficult time surviving, and probably won't, but you will save your soul. Again, don't take the mark on your right hand or forehead.

GEOPHYSICAL

In the gospel of Matthew, chapter 24, Jesus spoke to his disciples and indicated to them that one of the signs of the time of the end of the world would be, " . . . as it were in the days of Noah so will the coming of the son of man be." We read in Genesis that in the days of Noah "the earth was filled with violence.". This speaks not only of the violence that men inflict on one another—war, civil wars, rape, brutality, murder, abortion, and other indiscriminate, random acts of violence—but the earth itself is also filled with violence. We see increasing earthquakes, volcanoes, hurricanes, tornadoes, floods, drought, lightning storms and unusual atmospheric phenomena. While all of these have existed in the past, over the last 50 years, the number and intensity of these conditions and the property damage associated with these natural catastrophes has increased. As the level of violence that the human species has inflicted on one another has increased, so has the violent reaction of the earth increased.

SIGNS OF THE TIMES

When Jesus' disciples asked Him about the signs that would be a precursor to His coming and the end of the age His response, recorded in Matthew 24, was:

- Wars and rumors of wars
- Nation will rise against nation. It is very interesting to note that the Greek word that is translated as nation is "ethnos" which deals with ethnic background and race. Most of the wars and conflicts in the 1980's and 1990's are wars among ethnic groups and tribes.
- Kingdom will rise against kingdom
- Famines

- Earthquakes are "like the early pangs of childbirth. "As the time grows nearer and nearer to His coming, the frequency and intensity of these five signs will increase.
- The followers of Jesus will be handed over to be persecuted and killed. This is happening with more frequency in the Moslem controlled nations in the Middle East, and in Africa where Black Moslems are enslaving Black Christians.
- Christians will be hated by all nations on account of His name. In many parts of the world, Christians are jailed and killed for their beliefs; in the United States those who are Christians are hated by the media and liberals, and are known by the code words "religious right."
- Many will fall away . . . that is, many who claimed to be Christians will recant their faith, and betray and hate Christians.
- Many false prophets will arise and deceive many.
- Due to excessive lawlessness, the love of many will grow cold.

THE RAPTURE

This is an event that will not be hidden. The concept of the rapture has already been made known to the masses. It will be treated with ridicule, contempt and mockery by the world's media, but God will see to it that it will be highly publicized before it occurs just so that those left behind might still come to their senses. It will occur in the open, and everybody left behind will know someone who was raptured.

It will happen suddenly, unexpectedly, and lightning fast—"in the twinkling of an eye," as the Bible puts it. And there will be evidence all over the world that this event occurred. Some national leaders will disappear, celebrities in entertainment and professional sports will disappear, entire families will disappear, disbelieving spouses will see their mates vanish, children will disappear. Bank accounts, homes, cars, businesses and relationships will be left behind. The problem for the world's leaders will be trying to convince people that it didn't happen. Because if the world's leaders admit that it did happen then, logically, everything Christians preached about Jesus Christ being the Son of God, the Savior, the Messiah, the Prince of Peace, the Lord of Lords and King of Kings and everything that Jesus preached and taught must be true. And if all of this is true, then the only logical response would be to fall on one's knees before God in confession and repentance and absolute submission to every word of God (as revealed in the Bible). But all of this is diametrically opposed to the way of the world, which preaches freedom from the constraints of God's word, perverse sex, materialism and the devaluation of human life. So, although the rapture will shock everybody and will be covered in the media and everybody left will be aware of someone who is gone, the leaders of the world will begin their great deception, trying to convince the population left behind that there was no rapture.

How is this going to be accomplished? Well, pretty easily because most of the people left behind are already in a state of deception. They have been deceived into believing that Jesus is not the Messiah; they have been deceived into believing that the word of God is not true; they have been deceived into living a lifestyle that only brings constant pain and suffering instead of the freedom and paradise that God offers. The world's leaders will declare that there was no rapture, that a mass hysteria took place, and the news media will follow the party line. Then to make things easier, shortly after the rapture, one-fourth of the world's population will be decimated due to wars, famine and plague. Those who were raptured will be counted among the dead.

AFTER THE RAPTURE

Shortly after the rapture, a seven-year period known in the Bible as the Great Tribulation will take place. It will begin with the signing of a peace agreement between Israel and her enemies and it will end with the physical return of Jesus Christ to set up His kingdom on earth. In between, will be seven years of terror for those on earth. The following events and trends will take place in that seven-year period:

- A man will arise who will achieve victory after victory both in politics and in war(Rev 13:7). This man, who should be easily identified by his rapid rise and popularity, is your the anti-christ. Many people believe that this person must be Jewish. That is, in order for Jews to accept him as Messiah, only a Jew will suffice. This is not necessarily the case. The Bible does not specify that he is a Jew, and it does not specify nationality. Only God-fearing Jews will require a Jewish Messiah. The liberal, ungodly Jews who dominate Israel will be as lost when it comes to Biblical truth as the Gentiles of the world and will be deceived by his charisma, and more than likely, the desires of the world's media. Currently the new nickname for the United States is the Great Satan. This may have some significance.
- Violence will increase in all parts of the world, both nation against nation (ethnic wars) and domestically. Men will indiscriminately slay one another as peace will be removed from the earth (Rev 6:3-4).
- There will be extreme inflation, poverty, and lack of food as one day's wages will buy enough food for one day for one person (Rev 6:5-6).
- In a very short period of time, one-quarter of the earth's population will be killed due to wars, famine, pestilence and wild beasts. These wild beasts could very well be viruses, bacteria and other microbes. In late 1995, Time magazine ran a cover story on the rise of new infections and called microbes "malevolent little beasts" (Rev 6:7-8).
- Many people will experience a religious conversion and become followers of Jesus Christ and most of these people will be hunted down and killed (Dan 7:21).
- There will be a great earthquake, the sun will be blackened, the moon will turn red and all mountains and

islands (which are underwater mountains) will be moved (Joel 2:30-32).

- There will be a brief period of calm on the earth following this great earthquake which will give those who survive a false sense of security.
- One-third of the earth, one-third of all of trees and all the green grass will be burned up due to a comet or meteor that hits the earth (Rev 8:7).
- A meteor will hit the earth causing the sea to become like blood, killing one-third of all sea creatures and destroying one-third of all shipping (Rev 8:8-9).
- A "star" named Wormwood will fall from the sky and poison one-third of all fresh water killing many people (Rev 8:10-11).
- The sun, moon and stars will be darkened by one-third. The day and night will be reduced by one-third. There is some speculation that this means the rotation of the earth will be changed so that a day lasts only 16 hours instead of 24 hours (Rev 8:12).
- Fearsome locust-like beings will be released from underground who only attack people who are not followers of Jesus Christ. These attacks will be very painful but last only 5 months (Rev 9:1-11).
- An army of 200 million horse-like creatures will kill one-third of mankind (Rev 9:13-19).
- Two men (known as witnesses, see item 7 below) of Jewish origin will preach the Gospel of Jesus Christ for 3 1/2 years and be killed at the midpoint of the 7 year tribulation. These two will be responsible for a 3 1/2 year world-wide drought and will be killed by the anti-christ (also known as the beast in the Bible).
- People will be required to receive a mark on their right hand or forehead in order to buy and sell. Those who receive this mark will develop a loathsome and malignant sore on their bodies within a short period of time (Rev 13:13-18).

- The oceans will chemically change and become like the blood of a dead man (congealed?) and everything in the sea will die (Rev 16:3).
- The fresh waters will become like blood (Rev 16:4-7).
- The sun will scorch the people on earth with fierce heat (Rev 16:8-9).
- The throne of the anti-christ and his kingdom will become darkened (Rev 16:10-11).
- The Euphrates river will dry up allowing the kings of the east to march westward (Rev 16:12).
- The kings of the world will gather their armies together to battle God at Armageddon. There will be an earthquake so great that all of the mountains and islands will disappear. There will be hailstones weighing close to 100 pounds that will crush the armies that have gathered (Rev 16:17-22).
- Shortly after this great earthquake, Jesus Christ will return with His army to claim the earth as His possession (Zech 14:3-5).

THE TWO WITNESSES

These two men are God's gift to the people of the earth who refused to submit to the lordship of Jesus Christ prior to the rapture, but who will recognize the error in their life and seek God knowing the terrible mistake they have made. These two men will proclaim the gospel and provide hope for those left behind. Their message is for the salvation of the soul. They will have no message as to how you can avoid the hell that life on earth has become, because there is no hope to avoid that tribulation. If you are left on earth, then your destiny is to suffer and more than likely die. But you still have the hope of salvation. Listen to what these two men are preaching and turn to God.

The Bible does not say who these two men are. Many speculate that they are Elijah and Enoch, two ancient prophets of God who never died. Regardless, they will be responsible for many of the natural catastrophes that will wreak havoc on the property and economy of the earth. They will have the power to prevent rain, and there will be a 3 1/2 year drought on earth until they die. They will turn water into blood and cause all kinds of plagues on earth and, in general, make life miserable for those who are living on earth. Also, they will be invincible, as many will try to kill them only to be killed by their own hands. Those who attempt to blow them up will themselves be blown up; those who attempt to shoot them will have their guns explode in their hands; those who attempt to poison them will be poisoned by their own efforts. Only the world dictator will be able to kill them and only when God allows it.

The purpose of all the misery that these two witnesses inflict on the earth dwellers is to turn people back to God in repentance. The misery will be so great that when the world dictator does finally kill these two, the world will rejoice in a Christmas-like celebration, giving gifts to one another. Three and one-half days after their death they will be resurrected and, in full view of the entire population of the world, ascend to heaven at the command of God when He calls them to "Come up here." Shortly after he kills the two witnesses, the world dictator will declare himself to be God. He is the antichrist.

THE 144,000 JEWISH WITNESSES

Shortly after the rapture, God will call His army of 144,000 Jewish believers into service to provide a voice of hope for Jews throughout the world. The best friends and most staunch supporters of Jews have always been true, believing Christians. It was this element of the world's population that provided help and support for Israel and Jewish people. The rapture removed the Christian people from the earth and awakened the 144,000 to their purpose. These 144,000 preach to Jews worldwide that Jesus is the Messiah. These 144,000 will be spread out worldwide and more than likely go about in pairs, two by two, as Jesus instructed His disciples to do. It will be these 144,000 who will oppose Israel signing a peace treaty for protection; it will be the 144,000 who will identify the antichrist for who he is; it will be the 144,000 who will warn Israel of the treachery of the antichrist, and it will be the 144,000 who will lead the Jews worldwide to the hiding place prepared for them by God in the Judean desert. These 144,000 Jews are going to be strange people by normal standards: they will be celibate, very bold, fearless, and spiritually strong and probably very much like John the Baptist. You can read more about the 144,000 witnesses in Revelation 14.

MONEY

Hard currency will become obsolete. This is no surprise, as banks and governments have been working to eliminate currency, coin money and paper transactions for decades. Currency and coin is expensive to produce, lends itself readily for drug trafficking and, with high tech equipment, is too easily counterfeited. Banks desire to eliminate the teller position as an expense item, and with the elimination of paper checks and currency, all financial transactions can be handled with a computer. The debit card will become the tool for all personal financial transactions. However, at some point after the rapture, probably right after the two witnesses are killed, everyone will be required to get a mark on their right hand or forehead in order to buy and sell. Do not, do not, do not under any circumstances participate by receiving this mark. All those who receive this mark known as "the mark of the beast" are doomed for eternity. By taking this mark you are swearing allegiance to the anti-christ. You may as well attempt to enjoy life as best you can because eternity for you will be hell. It is at this point that God will have separated His followers from Satan's followers. Those who have taken the mark will persecute those without the mark. God will render judgment on those with the mark by inflicting them with a disgusting looking and very painful ulcer covering their bodies.

So how can a person without the mark survive and still buy and sell? Again, this will almost be impossible, but there will be people who are part of the anti-christ's regime who don't believe in the anti-christ; they are just "survivors" who pick the "winner" and seek to profit from that relationship. Therefore, save up for yourself gold; gold has always had value as money and always will, even in a cashless society. Identify one of these profiteers and seek to purchase food and living supplies from him. However, don't ever disclose to him how much gold you have and where it is. You want to be more valuable to him as a dealer than as a bounty. By the way, you will have a price on your head for not taking the mark. Obviously you won't be living an open life, as you will be in hiding somewhere at a remote location or in the forest on the outskirts of a large city. Your only goal will be to eat to live and hope to escape the militia hunting for you and those like you. Should you get caught, your fate will be either death or slavery.

If you receive this manual before the rapture and plan to be around after the rapture, then start storing up food and living supplies and put them into hiding in some remote and difficult to access area. You should include weaponry to defend yourself and medical supplies as part of your living supplies.

SAFETY CONCERNS

This era will be the most violent of times in the history of the world. Death, brutality and destruction will be part of everyday life. One of the defining characteristics of the last days following the rapture will be a lack of peace. There will be civil wars throughout the world: people will kill one another indiscriminately. Random acts of violence will fill people with fear. Car-jackings, home invasions, drive by shootings, and bombings will all increase with an intensity that will leave people with absolutely no sense of security.

In order to survive this time, you will need to remove yourself from society and live in a remote area that is difficult to access. Getting together with a group of like-minded people would provide additional support and safety.

As mentioned earlier, stock up on food, medicines, living supplies, weaponry and gold. You will need enough for 7 years. Don't plan on being able to supplement your food with hunting and fishing because the stocks of wild animals and fish will have been depleted and destroyed by the 3 1/2 year worldwide drought and three successive meteor-like or comet-like objects that strike the earth sometime after the rapture. The 3 1/2 year drought is brought on by the two witnesses. The first object from outer space to strike the earth will destroy 1/3 of all trees and all the green grass on earth. The second object, more like a meteor, strikes the sea and destroys 1/3 of all sea creatures and 1/3 of all shipping. The third object turns 1/3 of all fresh water poisonous and kills many people. Needless to say, all of this will also seriously deplete the food supplies for the world's population, causing food prices to skyrocket. Those people in the world who never before missed a meal or worried about food will become very familiar with hunger pangs and the feeling of going without food for long periods of time. This will be one of the causes of the increased violence as people become more self centered, short-tempered, and competitive for the food sources in short supply. As Jesus spoke to His disciples about these days, He said, "people will betray one another and hate one another . . . the love of many will grow cold."

HEALTH CONCERNS

Prior to the rapture, the world experienced an increase in health-related catastrophes, an increase in new infectious diseases and an increase in the return of diseases thought to have been eradicated or brought under control. The past two decades have brought on AIDS, EBOLA virus, flesh-eating bacteria, the return of tuberculosis, incurable gonorrhea, herpes and many other virtually incurable sexually transmitted diseases. After the rapture, things do not get better, as one quarter of the world's population will die as the result of wars, famine and plague. Sometime after the two witnesses are murdered and after people are required to take the mark on the right hand or forehead, there will be a terrible plague causing a loathsome and malignant ulcer on the bodies of those who have taken the mark. This will be a very ugly and very painful sore that will make life miserable for those who have it.

In addition to all this, because of the poor economic situation worldwide and the 3 1/2 year drought that depletes the world's supply of water, sanitation practices will deteriorate even in what were advanced nations in Europe and North America. With the short supply of water, there won't be sufficient water for flushing toilets, taking baths, washing clothes and transporting wastewater to treatment facilities. This will result in the increase of typhus, cholera, salmonella and E.coli infections.

Therefore, since you have decided to reject Christ's offer to join in the rapture, your concern is how to maintain good health in the post rapture era. You must build a supply of multiple vitamins with particular emphasis on anti-oxidants such as C and E and minerals. It will also be necessary to have a supply of disinfectants, particularly one that can be added to water to make it potable.

Above all, do not accept the mark of the beast on your right hand or forehead. If you do take the mark then nothing can be done for you—you will suffer the malignant ulcer making the rest of your life almost unbearable. Did you ever have a canker sore in your mouth? If so, then you know how painful that one little canker sore was. Now think of having canker sores all over your body, on your genitalia, in your mouth. Think how painful and unbearable your life will be. Then follow that misery with eternity in hell. Don't take that mark.

INDEX OF WORKS CITED

"Heaven has no rage like love to hatred turned/ Nor hell a fury like a woman scorned." **by <u>William Congreve</u> in *The Mourning Bride* of 1697.**

Matthew 24:34-42 (King James Version)

[6]Set me as a seal upon thine heart, as a seal upon thine arm: for love is strong as death; jealousy is cruel as the grave: the coals thereof are coals of fire, which hath a most vehement flame. [7]Many waters cannot quench love; neither can the floods drown it: if a man would give all the substance of his house for love, it would utterly be contemned. **Song of Solomon 8:6-7 (King James Version)**

<u>The Feathers of Ma 'at</u> by Liquid Poetry

<u>Truth</u> (Lyrics from CD) **by EboniSkye**

<u>THE POST RAPTURE SURVIVAL GUIDE</u> by Kurt Seland

ABOUT THE AUTHOR

M. Lewis Ryan was born in Houston Texas. She is a graduate of Texas Southern University, a member of the National Association of Professional Women, and a Christian Sociologist. Early in life her parents, Joan and Lucien Lewis II, discovered their daughter was blessed with the God giving talent for writing poetry, drawing and painting. She began performing at a number of local poetry bars under the stage name of EboniSkye. She is currently working on giving back to God, that which He so graciously gave her. She is writing  inspirational poetry books, novels, making cd, painting and starting a greeting card line by EboniSkye. Mrs. Ryan's goal is to teach the world about Jesus Christ by using her life as an example and showing how to obtain salvation through faith and the blood of Jesus Christ. Contemned was written as an inspiration book and a check point for her readers to stop and evaluated where they are in life from where they need to be in their Christian walk with Jesus. It allows the reader an opportunity to know the Lord God and offers a gentle guide towards truth and understanding of the rapture. Spoken Words of EboniSkye was M. Lewis Ryan first book published by Author House. She expresses her excitement in sharing many more in the near future.

Look for her new cd: "Truth" and help support the charities: Food For Life INC, Sacred Seniors and Sacred Minds of America INC with the purchase of any of her products, M. Lewis Ryan donates $1.00 towards one of these three charities. Help Us Help Others.

Thank You and God Bless You,

EboniSkye